"Heidi Diouf brings a lot of warmth, wit, and wisdom to her writing and teaching and has a knack for helping others to recognize their unknown Superpowers. If you are looking to turn up the volume on the positives in your life, The Superpower Playbook will be a great tool for discovering your Superpower(s) and putting them to good use in your work and your relationships with yourself and others."

—Laura Burian,
Professor of Chinese/ English Translation & Interpretation, Middlebury Institute of International Studies at Monterey; Professional musician

The Superpower Playbook reminds us about what ignites our Superpower: being of service to others. I highly recommend this book to amplify your Superpower to its greatest degree for the highest good of yourself and the world. Heidi gives you the tools to empower your thoughts and breakthrough limitations to get there."

—Caterina Rando,
Founder: Thriving Women in Business Community Publisher: Thriving Women in Business Magazine, author *Learn to Power Think*

"If you are wanting to "Unlock Your Superpowers" and play a bigger game in your life and work, grab a copy of Heidi Diouf's *Superpower Playbook*. In it, she guides you on a journey of self-discovery that will enable you to tap into your genius and ignite your passion for making positive changes in your life. It's a powerful read!"

—Jane Deuber,
CEO of Global Experts Accelerator and Founder of Smart Biz Quiz

"*The Superpower Playbook* inspires you to break free of limiting mindsets so you can channel the strength of your Superpower(s). Heidi guides you to align with your next Superpower level of being."

—Nicole DeAvilla,
author of *The 2 Minute Yoga Solution*

"Heidi's *Superpower Playbook* opened my eyes to my actual Superpower, which I would not have guessed. And, gave me some specific strategies on how to embrace my Superpower and welcome more of it in to my life. If you've been curious about a highly valuable part of yourself that you may be overlooking, I encourage you to read this book and discover more of yourself and the Superpower you may be taking for granted."

—Alexis Neely, Founder
New Law Business Model &
Eyes Wide Open Life
http://www.LawBusinessMentors.com
http://www.EyesWideOpenLife.com

"Heidi's exploration into the different Superpower archetypes is a fresh and relevant take on identifying our strengths so that we can be more available to the larger needs of the time."

—Light Watkins,
Author of *Bliss More & The Inner Gym*

THE SUPERPOWER PLAYBOOK

THE SUPERPOWER PLAYBOOK

Heidi Diouf

Copyright © 2017 by Heidi Diouf

Title: The Superpower Playbook

Printed in United States of America

ISBN: 978-0-9994616-2-4

Publishing company name: JAI Ganesha Press

This book is designed to provide information and motivation to our readers. It is sold with the understanding that the publisher is not engaged to render any type of psychological, legal, or any other kind of professional advice. The content of each article is the sole expression and opinion of its author, and not necessarily that of the publisher. No warranties or guarantees are expressed or implied by the publisher's choice to include any of the content in this volume. Neither the publisher nor the individual author(s) shall be liable for any physical, psychological, emotional, financial, or commercial damages, including, but not limited to, special, incidental, consequential or other damages. Our views and rights are the same: You are responsible for your own choices, actions, and results.

DEDICATION

For all people to come together in peaceful unity activating our Superpowers for the highest and greatest healing good of our communities and the earth.

A portion of the profits from this book are donated to the Senegal Health Institute: www.senegalhealth.org. The Senegal Health Institute is a non-profit organization dedicated to improving the general health and well-being of impoverished women, children, and families in the villages of the Casamance region of Senegal by providing stable health care services, safe birthing practices, and reproductive health and family planning education. Another portion of the profits will be donated to The Power of Love Women Entrepreneurs Program: www.sharednation.org helps African women whose families have been impacted by AIDS/HIV. They provide business training and microloans so these women can financially support their families.

FOREWORD

As I reflect on the words of *The Superpower Playbook*, I notice how words become influential: how they compel us to action, feeling, and movement. Heidi's Superpower campaign resonates with my pursuit to teach health and wellness and motivates me to continue. Love is central to conquering fear, and we, as leaders in our respective movements, keep a pulse on love while driving others to attain their unlimited potential. As teachers of yoga, we tap into breath and awareness and allow them to be our guide. As writers, we rely on words to reveal buried obstacles. As coaches of healthy lifestyles, we support methods that groove with our clients. In all my modes of being, Heidi and I resonate with each other on many levels, and I am honored to support her movement.

To navigate the dance with fear and failure, we need to become our action heroines. Heidi and I will share insights about using the power of *now* to change our thoughts, actions, and beliefs to propel people to move beyond their limitations. As you can find in my book, *Beautiful Money,* Heidi and I complement our approaches by making space to receive what you truly desire. I invite our combined followers to use this space to activate your highest potential in love, leadership, leverage, and legacy. Heidi urges you to actualize your Superpowers and energize your core virtues to lead you to your highest potential. As you gaze inward and evaluate your life through the Superpower lens, you will allow your most prosperous self to emerge and light the passage to your next stage of evolution. The Superpower Playbook is a joyful reminder that trusting our inner power is the secret to pursuing our highest visions. I am in love with the wisdom and philosophy Heidi has to offer.

—Leanne Jacobs, Founder of HealthyGirl, author of *Beautiful Money.*

CONTENTS

Prologue — xi

Chapter 1	What is a Superpower?	1
Chapter 2	The Activator: Celebrate inspired action	19
Chapter 3	The Amplifier: Celebrate Having a Volume Dial	24
Chapter 4	The Observer: Celebrate the Big Picture	29
Chapter 5	The Transformer: Celebrate Metamorphosis	34
Chapter 6	The Innovator: Celebrate Modification	40
Chapter 7	The Expander: Celebrate stretching beyond limits	45
Chapter 8	The Container: Celebrate Systems	50
Chapter 9	The Synthesizer: Celebrate Harmony	54
Chapter 10	The Empath: Celebrate Walking in Another's Shoes	59
Chapter 11	The Limitless Achiever: Celebrate Goals	64
Chapter 12	The Optimist: Celebrate Positivity	69
Chapter 13	The Intuitive: Celebrate internal guidance	74

Chapter 14	Managing Fear	80
Chapter 15	How to Approach Failure	92
Chapter 16	Adding and Combining Superpowers	102
Chapter 17	Core Virtues	111
Chapter 18	Importance of Integration	121
Chapter 19	Breakthrough	126
Acknowledgements		146
Bibliography		147
Resources		148

PROLOGUE

*Tell me, what is it you plan to do with your
one wild and precious life?*

—Mary Oliver

I came up with the idea for this book while grinding coffee beans. My most profound insights usually reveal themselves when I am performing mundane tasks. These sudden ideas make me stop in my tracks – I eagerly grab my phone and hit the record button so I can remember the thought.

While making my coffee, I was thinking about how I could form a close-knit fellowship with my new yoga students during our daylong retreat. I had spent the week leading up to the event with my cousin, Mary Ann, who has a knack for getting personal information from random people in less than five minutes. She has a particular way of making people feel immediately at ease. I told her that her Superpower was her curiosity, combined with her invisible "Wonder-Woman truth lasso." I proposed to my students that each one of them had a Superpower and described my cousin as an example. Their challenge was to discover Superpowers in each other by the end of the day. To their surprise, every student found a Superpower in one another during the retreat.

When I introduced the idea of Superpowers, I had a revelation. Many people did not realize they had a Superpower, nor did they know how to use one. My yoga retreat circle sparkled with excitement at the notion of *having* a Superpower. The "Superpower Challenge" transformed the newcomers into a bonded community.

While I was writing this book, extreme political division left my country distraught. The controversial election and national conflict reflected in my yoga students and clients in my intuitive coaching practice. It was disconcerting. Hiking became my stress reliever each day. As I hiked, I would receive what I call "spontaneous downloads" for each chapter of this book. Bringing the day's current questions to an inspiring, natural setting, I found myself mapping insights about Superpowers. I was moved to write a playbook to reach a wider audience than the people I interacted with in my small business. I wanted this book to inspire people to act *with* their Superpower to bring people together. As the book unfolded, I began seeing Superpowers in everyday people. My discoveries led me to interview people who actively represented a specific Superpower. Then, the realization hit me: we can access **all** of our Superpowers.

There are multiple Superpowers we access in all the different roles we play. As a mother, I have used many to navigate each developmental stage for my daughter. Several Superpowers are activated in my intuitive coaching practice to support and motivate my clients toward polishing their Superpowers. Meanwhile, my students and clients foster my Superpower growth. By encouraging people to use their innate gifts *and* develop new Superpowers opens new pathways to a more significant evolution of consciousness. In my process of teaching yoga and developing intuition, I gained a deeper insight about applying Superpowers in various contexts. When we follow our inner guidance, it shows us when and how we are in alignment. I want this book to remind us how we are all connected in some way.

Let my words be of service and support to you in actualizing your highest purpose. Remember, all the Superpowers do reside within you. Allow the exercises, affirmations, and meditations to inspire and instill confidence, boosting your aptitude for greatness—and supporting others to do the same.

My Superpower Story

It was December 2003, and I was sitting, exhausted, on the floor of my friend's brand-new office. We had finished moving her boxes in and setting up the reception area. Linda was an acupuncturist, healer, and wise woman. Our friendship had blossomed since 2000. We had met in Monterey and realized we both moved from the San Francisco Bay area around the same time. Our views on holistic health, meditation, and lifestyle aligned. I felt happy for her as she had finally landed the perfect place to grow her practice. As we were sitting on the floor, feeling accomplished, she mentioned recently feeling soreness in her abdomen, which came and went. Instantly, I had a sick feeling in the pit of my stomach, too. My gut told me her pain was from cancer. I sat there silently, doubting my intuition —my "doubt monster" talking me out of sharing my hunch with Linda. *Linda is healthy... she does cleanses... takes herbs...does hot yoga... exercises.... meditates... does Tai Chi. There is NO WAY your intuition is valid.*

I said nothing.

Fast forward a month later to mid-January, 2004, she was treating me for pneumonia with acupuncture. When I saw her, I experienced the same gut feeling, but this time it was overwhelming. *It's cancer. Tell her.* But my doubt monster piped back up: *You're tired. You aren't clear.* (I was exhausted from taking care of my 22-month-old-baby who refused to sleep through the night.) Again, I let fear and doubt silence my intuitive voice.

A week later, Linda got an ultrasound. She called to tell me her diagnosis: pancreatic cancer, now in an advanced stage. She chose diet, herbs, and acupuncture to help her body heal but knew her prognosis did not encourage a full recovery. Her family, friends, and I spent the next three months supporting her and keeping her comfortable until her death. I never told her what I sensed that day in her office.

Many months later, I was helping her husband go through her things and grieving with him. I told him about my gut feeling in her office. I waited for his wrath. I figured I deserved it. Instead, he told me that pancreatic cancer is aggressive and difficult to overcome.

"It's not your fault," he reassured me. He didn't blame me, or hold me accountable. The hardest part was forgiving myself. From that day forward, I promised myself to speak up every time I got a hunch about someone's health—to never again fret about being wrong.

A few years later, a regular client, Gloria, came in for bodywork and I got that feeling again. *She has cancer.* My fears and doubts resurfaced, but this time I urged her to go to the doctor for a scan. I didn't sleep that night. I called her the next morning to say, "Go to the doctor now."

Gloria called me back the next day to tell me the doctors did indeed find a tumor. She needed to have surgery immediately. Thankfully, Gloria survived and chose to make healthy changes to her lifestyle. Since then, I have worked with many people with varying degrees of mental, physical, and emotional imbalances. I now ignore my doubts or fears and speak up.

My big takeaway from this experience to others is to trust yourself. My Superpower of intuition lets me be of service. Denying my gift or downplaying its importance served no one. Instead, denial only created pain. As Marianne Williamson wrote in *Return to Love*, "Our deepest fear is not that we are inadequate. Our deepest fear is that we are powerful beyond measure. It is our light, not our darkness, that most frightens us. We ask ourselves, 'Who am I to be brilliant, gorgeous, talented, fabulous?' Actually, who are you not to be? You are a child of God. You're playing small does not serve the world."

I allowed my fear of my light—my Superpower, to overshadow my love for a friend. When we devalue ourselves with thoughts like, "who am *I* to even *HAVE* a Superpower?", we limit everyone's possibilities for light, love, and power.

Our Superpowers are innate gifts. I believe they are meant to be appreciated, grown, nurtured, and shared. Even though we may be our own best saboteurs, we would do better to use Superpowers for the highest good. I wrote this book to ignite you and those around you to initiate positive change in alignment with your Superpower gifts. I want to embolden you to attack life's challenges *with* your Superpowers, rather than hide from them with fear or shame.

So, I ask you, who are you NOT to have Superpowers? How could it possibly serve you and others to hold back your Superpowers?

CHAPTER 1

WHAT IS A SUPERPOWER?

"Potential is a priceless treasure, like gold. All of us have gold hidden within, but we have to dig to get it out."

—Joyce Meyer

I define a Superpower as a stand-out, inherent quality you can activate to achieve a desired outcome.

We all witnessed Superpowers in the Olympics in many ways. Michael Phelps expressed his Superpower by inspiring children to dream big with swimming. The media published an old photo with Michael and a 10-year-old boy from Singapore named Joseph Schooling to promote youth competitive swimming. That pivotal meeting motivated the little boy to train passionately. Nine years later, he beat Phelps, his hero, at the summer Olympics to win the gold medal in the 100-meter Butterfly. Phelps is what I call (in Chapter 2) an "Activator." While Joseph Schooling became a "Limitless Achiever." (Chapter 11)

Another dramatic example of Superpowers at the Olympics was the 5,000-meter race, where two runners, Abbey D'Agostino from the USA, and Nikki Hamblin from New Zealand, collided and fell. Abbey stopped to lift Nikki up, urging her back into the race, as she felt empathy for her fellow competitor. Afterward, Nikki helped Abbey off the track because she needed medical attention. As Abbey displayed attributes of the "Empath"(Chapter 10) and the "Optimist."(Chapter 12) Nikki became the "Limitless Achiever." They revealed they could move beyond the pressure to win medals, becoming heroes to one another and the world. These athletes showed others that despite fierce competition, altruism could bring elite athletes together. One small Superpower-driven act can affect global levels of compassion and understanding.

My curiosity about Superpowers led me to interview everyday people who used their powers in different contexts. I started with Steve, a professional business consultant. Steve had 30 years of experience coaching corporate leaders of Fortune 500 companies, and he offered some clues about how large corporations could activate Superpowers. He observed a pattern in corporate teams: they rushed to complete projects with overly ambitious deadlines, but many team leaders overlooked the value of cultivating a truly cohesive unit. Consequently, Steve created strategies to help them discover their unique talents. When team members focused on giving support to one another, they felt empowered, and the team yielded far more fruitful outcomes. Valuing Superpowers generated synthesis and success.

We can gain far greater outcomes when we invest time to develop our strengths, and by supporting others to do the same. I remember times when I was on the swimming and cross-country teams preparing for a big game or meet. It was exhilarating to cheer on a team member that was performing at their best. It felt good when our team shattered a state record. All of our shared experiences of working out, eating together, and going out socially created a strong bond. My teammates motivated me to run my best races and swim my best times. Can you think of a time in which you worked with a group seeking a goal? The time invested training together was critical. Remember how valuable your input was to the group's accomplishment? If you were to take yourself out of the picture, how would the outcome have differed?

As you examine what people ask of you in different contexts, it can also direct you toward your Superpower discovery. If you received accolades or awards, contemplate what it took to win them. Think about how many times you received recognition for the same action. Recall how you were recognized. What words did people use to describe you as they handed a trophy or award to you?

Ultimately, what you are reading is a SELF-LOVE book, not a self-help book. I believe you already *have* these Superpowers in you. I am writing the following to show you how to first recognize, then turn up the volume on your strengths—and encourage others to amplify theirs—to help you strengthen relationships, live your best life, and help others live theirs.

Superpower Questionnaire

I developed this questionnaire to help you best determine your *dominant* Superpower, as well as others you may already access. Please read all the options before selecting **ONE** that best describes you. While several options may resonate, try choosing the one that speaks to you first. There are 20 questions with 12 answer choices. The questionnaire should take around 15-20 minutes to complete.

1. ***How do you think of time?***
   a) *I never have enough to do all the things I want to do.*
   b) *I look at time as cyclical. I decide where I want to focus most of my energy for each cycle.*
   c) *I like to have time in my week to relax, look at nature, or people-watch.*
   d) *My idea of time changes depending on where I am at with life. Time ebbs and flows with whatever I am doing.*
   e) *When I am engrossed in a creative project, I lose track of time.*
   f) *I avoid the pressure of feeling limited with time as much as possible. I want to be free of any parameters or schedules.*
   g) *I like a regular, planned schedule.*
   h) *I prefer to have plenty of time to do what I want so I can remain peaceful. I don't like to feel rushed or stressed.*
   i) *I tend to keep my schedule and beliefs about time separate from those around me. I avoid being around those whose beliefs make me feel stressed about time.*
   j) *I know that time is limited so I am efficient with the time I have. I keep to a schedule of what needs to be done so I can ensure reaching my goals on time.*

k) *I see time as a continuous stream of positive experiences. I have plenty of time for everything.*
l) *I tune in to the present moment, sensing what actions would best serve me now.*

2. When I first see a new product trending, I...

a) *just buy it—I like to be the first to test it out.*
b) *decide if the product will make life easier and create more output with less time or resources.*
c) *wait till others have tried it and evaluate their results.*
d) *figure out if the product will relieve my current stress and create positive changes or outcomes.*
e) *evaluate if I can tweak something I already have for the same results.*
f) *make a list of pros and cons to assess if the product can expand my current experience.*
g) *research if there are similar quality products that are less expensive on the market.*
h) *wonder if this product would be helpful to people I know.*
i) *imagine myself using the product and see if it resonates.*
j) *research whether this product will be efficient.*
k) *evaluate whether this product will improve what I already love to do.*
l) *trust my gut feeling about the effectiveness of this product for my life.*

3. When you are on public transportation, what do you do?

a) *I join in a casual conversation with friendly people.*
b) *I notice what people are talking about.*
c) *I watch people and make up stories about them.*
d) *I allow my curiosity to draw me into a conversation.*
e) *I think of how public transportation could be improved so I could get to my destination faster.*
f) *I enjoy listening to conversations around me to hear what is new and expand my knowledge.*

g) *I seat myself where I can get grounded and centered.*
h) *I gravitate to a person/group that seems peaceful.*
i) *I get overwhelmed on public transportation because I feel all the emotions of the environment.*
j) *I sit near the front so I can be the first one off and get to my destination quickly.*
k) *I talk to the person next to me if they are friendly.*
l) *I look for a single seat so I can rest and meditate.*

4. **When I am at a party, I prefer to...**

   a) *chat with lots of people and make sure I encourage everyone to talk about themselves.*
   b) *turn up the music, pour the wine, and get the good times going whenever there's a lull.*
   c) *find a good spot to sit back and take it all in.*
   d) *keep the conversation flowing by changing up the subjects when conversation wanes.*
   e) *take mental notes on everything from food, to lighting, for the next party I throw.*
   f) *seek out the most colorful personalities in the room to talk to.*
   g) *see if the host needs a hand, then settle in and get cozy.*
   h) *start a game to get people together.*
   i) *speak to a few people and tune into how they express themselves.*
   j) *meet as many people as I can.*
   k) *kick back, have fun and make people laugh.*
   l) *seek out like-minded people for interesting conversations.*

5. **When I am brainstorming to help a friend or colleague, I like to...**

   a) *think of one to two simple actions that could motivate them.*
   b) *think of ways I could amplify their talent or qualities by offering suggestions.*

c) listen with neutrality to give them a big-picture perspective of what I observe is happening.
   d) listen to their ideas and offer different possibilities they have not yet considered.
   e) help them evaluate pros and cons.
   f) give plenty of options not yet considered.
   g) be spontaneous and come up with ideas based on their needs.
   h) be collaborative and come up with ideas that create more harmony with their desired outcome.
   i) give them space to be emotional, but keep them on task to solve the problem.
   j) come up with a game plan with measurable steps, leading to their goal.
   k) be positive and supportive.
   l) share helpful ideas that first come to mind.

6. **When I start a creative project, the first action item on my list is…**
   a) a list? I don't need one—I will figure it out as I go.
   b) to see what materials I need to make this better than the picture on the box/magazine.
   c) think about the project as a whole, then make a plan.
   d) evaluate how I want this project to change what I already have now.
   e) see if I can use any of my current materials in a different way to get the desired result.
   f) go on Pinterest to gather ideas and see how I can add flair to the project.
   g) create a timeline.
   h) think about how the project can be done comfortably without rushing.
   i) imagine how I want to feel when this project is complete.
   j) set a deadline.
   k) evaluate what parts of the project are easy or difficult.
   l) intuit where I can get resources for this project.

7. ***I am moving to a new house in a new location I have never been to before so I...***
   a) *think of it as an adventure. I can't wait to pack!*
   b) *look forward to making new friends.*
   c) *start investigating what the community is like by finding a good people-watching spot.*
   d) *am eager (I was longing for variety.)*
   e) *look at the places in the new community that interest me and list all the possibilities of how this move will improve my life.*
   f) *make a list of all the things I want to learn and do in this new place.*
   g) *can't wait to remodel the house and make it mine.*
   h) *research the community to see what groups interest me so I can connect with like-minded people.*
   i) *explore the community places that interest me and gauge the vibe of people's interactions.*
   j) *want to move in immediately and start my new life; I will figure out the details later.*
   k) *look at the bright side. I'm eager for the new experiences and friendships awaiting me.*
   l) *will notice the hunches I pick up on the place, people, and community when I visit.*

8. ***If I am leading a group project with a deadline I...***
   a) *like to spark ideas into action immediately.*
   b) *evaluate everyone's skill set/experience then delegate tasks to people fitting each need.*
   c) *observe everyone's contributions during the project-planning, then offer ideas for collaboration.*
   d) *offer possibilities to create an approach to match the desired outcome.*

e) ask team members about their past relevant experiences, then offer suggestions about applying their talents.
f) survey the group to brainstorm different ways the project could be successful.
g) make lists of the tasks, materials, and deadline. I make a rough outline, prioritizing what needs to be done sequentially, then present the project to the group.
h) figure out how to get people to work with cohesion given their skill set and experience.
i) evaluate others' responses to the project presentation to sense how they could contribute.
j) present the project with a sign-up sheet so tasks get done efficiently.
k) give an upbeat project presentation, then ask team members to contribute what they do best.
l) journal and meditate on how I can best serve as a leader. I log the first ideas, then follow this guidance as I present suggestions to the group.

9. *When I am fearful of uncertain outcomes I...*

a) just move forward and avoid thinking about my fear. If I stop and give my energy to fear, it will slow me down.
b) complete some activity that amplifies my confidence and strength, drowning out my fear and putting me in a positive frame of mind.
c) research how others in similar circumstances approached my situation, then make an action plan.
d) sit with the current situation and breathe to calm my emotions, then allow myself to think of all the ways I could change my approach to achieve my desired result.
e) strategize how I could take some uncertainty out of the outcome. I try the first idea that comes to me; if it doesn't work, I try the next idea with some modifications.

f) make lists of various paths to several possible outcomes. I surround myself in nature to clear my mind.

g) research similar scenarios, evaluating what would work for me. I then make a task timeline.

h) gather a team of talented people who can brainstorm through the uncertainty and encourage me to face my fear.

i) talk to close friends to get their feedback. I go with the plan that makes me feel most peaceful.

j) do not believe in fear. I set my mind on the most favorable outcome and take measured risks and calculated steps to get there.

k) put my best foot forward and figure I will eventually get more confident as I progress. I am grateful for the opportunity to grow.

l) trust my gut feelings about how to respond every step of the way. I look at my fear objectively and focus on progress instead.

10. When I want a new job, or change in my current employment status I…

a) immediately look for the job and start putting out my resume that week.

b) see how I can turn up the volume on one of my strengths that fits the job I desire.

c) go to a possible workplace and watch the everyday happenings to see if it's a fit.

d) change something about myself OR change something at my workplace so that I am happier at my current job.

e) suggest modifications to my current position and show how this change will improve the company.

f) make a list of all the pros and cons of my current job, then explore if there is a better place to match my needs.

g) organize and update my resume as well as online social media profiles to attract my desired position.

h) think of all the ways I can attract the job I want with gratitude and a positive attitude, then make progress each day.

    i)   talk to people who work at a different place and notice if their feelings resonate with mine.
    j)   make a list of all I want to contribute, then set a goal and deadline to find the right position.
    k)   start thinking about intriguing jobs that I have not tried yet. Affirm the right job for me with positive thoughts, then put out my resume.
    l)   think about the benefits of staying in my current job and tune into possibilities of finding something better.

11. I want to learn a new skill in an area that intrigues, yet intimidates me. I approach it by...

    a)   jumping in with focused curiosity. No hesitation.
    b)   taking stock of all my current skills and tapping into courage. I focus on what I am, instead of what I am not.
    c)   observing others and choosing a skill I can master.
    d)   changing my mindset and learning the new skill with complete trust.
    e)   researching what others have done to achieve it. I think about all the applications of that skill and am open to the process.
    f)   having a beginner's mindset and listing all the conventional and creative ways I can learn the skill.
    g)   researching all aspects of the skill. Then I list what I need to learn and prepare a routine to do so.
    h)   learning the skill in a beginning class with a forgiving teacher in a comfortable environment.
    i)   taking a group class to see how I feel trying it.
    j)   making it a goal to learn it, then taking measured steps to master it.
    k)   attuning my attitude to positivity—I can do anything when I put my mind to it.
    l)   trusting my guidance about what I need to do, then visualizing my next step to achieving it.

12. **How do you approach failure?**

    a) I think of failure as an unexpected result but avoid placing a negative label on it. I change my approach if my first attempt did not meet expectations.

    b) I think about achieving a different outcome by adding or subtracting actions and attitudes.

    c) I step back from my emotional reaction to the current outcome to gain a larger perspective. I change my plan of action to match this new perspective.

    d) I can change my mind about the current outcome and accept it or I can change my steps toward getting a more acceptable result.

    e) Back to the drawing board—I can try another modification to get a better result.

    f) I expand my approach with more possibilities to achieve a better outcome.

    g) I have a few backup plans if my first approach does not go as planned. I systematically try each one until I get the outcome I want.

    h) I collaborate with others attempting a similar goal and tap into their ideas.

    i) I try something different by choosing an approach that resonates with my gut feeling.

    j) I do not believe in failure. I believe I got a result I did not expect. I will alter my plan of attack.

    k) I think of it as an opportunity to recreate myself.

    l) Failure is just an outcome I did not expect. I trust my intuition to guide me to a different choice yielding a more desirable result.

13. **What are the top two traits that best describe you?**

    a) Motivated and Decisive
    b) Charismatic and Warm
    c) Observant and Thoughtful
    d) Spontaneous and Flowing
    e) Inventive and Original

f) Boundless and Open-minded
g) Grounded and Organized
h) Friendly and Inclusive
i) Sensitive and Receptive
j) Focused and Intense
k) Enthusiastic and Buoyant
l) Perceptive and Instinctual

14. How does being of service give you a sense of peace and fulfillment?

a) By encouraging others to take inspired action toward their goals.
b) By increasing a friend or colleague's confidence in strengths that they have not yet actualized.
c) By offering valuable, life-improving information to others from a neutral perspective.
d) By helping others realize that positive change is attainable.
e) By modifying life to make it better for myself and others.
f) By offering limitless possibilities that grant others hope.
g) By creating achievable systems that make it easier for people to navigate their life with clarity.
h) By ensuring that everyone feels peaceful when they are in a community.
i) By helping individuals feel at peace with themselves.
j) By inspiring others to release limitations and become their best self.
k) By uplifting people to feel happy about who they are.
l) By helping people tune into their internal guidance that serves their most fulfilling purpose.

15. Which of your qualities are you most grateful for?

a) My confidence.
b) My warmth.
c) My perspective.

d) *My adaptability.*
e) *My resourcefulness.*
f) *My boundless ideas.*
g) *My discipline.*
h) *My peacefulness.*
i) *My sensitivity.*
j) *My incentive.*
k) *My attitude.*
l) *My guidance.*

16. *How do you make decisions?*

a) *With efficiency, confidence, and certainty.*
b) *With courage—once I know that I have enough energy to follow through with all the steps involved in the decision.*
c) *With careful research of all aspects that could be impacted by the decision.*
d) *With excitement and eagerness because I love to see how the decision influences change.*
e) *With faith that the conclusion is impermanent—I can change my approach if I want to alter the results.*
f) *With flexibility—if it does not pan out the way I expect I can try a different path.*
g) *With grounded certainty because I researched and planned for the outcome.*
h) *With a comfortable amount of time devoted to weighing all possible consequences—I don't like to rush into quick decisions.*
i) *With reflection, then checking in with my gut feeling about what direction I should choose.*
j) *With ease and quickness because I do not like to waste time vacillating. I am confident I can handle any outcome.*
k) *With conviction because I have a positive attitude and can accept any outcome.*
l) *In alignment with my inner guidance.*

17. How do you become absorbed in something new in your life? (relationship, job, hobby, interest)

   a)   *By immediately immersing myself in it.*
   b)   *By fine-tuning my gifts that will enhance it.*
   c)   *By seeing it from different angles.*
   d)   *By merging with it, allowing it to change me.*
   e)   *By letting go of any attachment to outcome.*
   f)   *By embracing it and logging all insights I get along the way.*
   g)   *By measured and repeated steps that become routine.*
   h)   *By learning and sharing it with others.*
   i)   *By "testing the waters" to see how it feels.*
   j)   *By doing it repeatedly, every day. I sync with it.*
   k)   *By engaging with positive thoughts and enthusiasm.*
   l)   *By immersing myself in it and observing my intuition in the process.*

18. How do you solve problems?

   a)   *By initiating a course of action to create a different result.*
   b)   *By revising my approach. I add or subtract any emotional factors that will affect the outcome.*
   c)   *By reevaluating it from a big picture perspective.*
   d)   *By evaluating how the problem blocks my transformation, then changing my course of action.*
   e)   *By trial and error, modifying something different each time.*
   f)   *By expanding my perspective of the problem. There may be a benefit I have not considered.*
   g)   *By trying one of my back up plans.*
   h)   *By adapting to a different approach I have not tried that feels comfortable.*
   i)   *By tuning into what feels incongruent about the problem, then reevaluating my choices to solve it.*

j) *By prioritizing the problem then trying creative solutions.*

k) *By seeing the problem as the potential for growth. I embrace the situation as a powerful learning experience.*

l) *By listening to my initial hunch on changing my approach to achieve the best solution.*

19. **How do you feel about deadlines?**

    a) *I generally do not need them because I am motivated to complete tasks that will get me there efficiently.*

    b) *They keep me present and focused on what I need to do now.*

    c) *I need deadlines or I may get distracted daydreaming.*

    d) *I prefer deadlines because they help me map out changes along the way. I like to mark my progress.*

    e) *I rely on deadlines; otherwise, I lose track of time.*

    f) *I dislike deadlines. They bring pressure, and I prefer to create without looking at the clock.*

    g) *I prefer staying on a schedule and making deadlines for each task that lead to completion.*

    h) *I need deadlines. Although they do not always feel easy, they keep me on target.*

    i) *I can work with deadlines easily because I can tune into what I need to do to make each step happen.*

    j) *I see deadlines as steps toward reaching my goals. I love getting things done ahead of schedule.*

    k) *I accept deadlines as a part of life and I do my best to keep them.*

    l) *Deadlines help me prioritize the tasks needed to achieve the goal.*

20. **How do you spend your solitary leisure time?**

    a) *Being active, either physically and/or mentally with exercise or learning.*

    b) *Relaxing with a repetitive hobby.*

    c) *People-watching or going to museums.*

d) Doing activities or going places that are new and different.
e) Doing anything where I am not bound by time.
f) Going somewhere in nature where I can see an expansive vista.
g) Clearing clutter, reorganizing or redecorating a space in my house.
h) Working in the garden, getting my hands in the dirt.
i) Writing a note or reaching out to a close friend.
j) Exercising physically or mentally to strengthen myself.
k) Watching the sun come up and enjoying nature.
l) Meditating in nature and/or writing in a journal.

Tally your selected responses by letter:

8 or more of one letter = This is your dominant Superpower.
6-7 = You have strong inclinations of this Superpower.
3-5 = You have traces of this Superpower.
Less than 3-5 = You are all over the map. It means you have a smattering of all the Superpowers, depending on the circumstances.

a. The Activator
b. The Amplifier
c. The Observer
d. The Transformer
e. The Innovator
f. The Expander
g. The Container
h. The Synthesizer
i. The Empath
j. The Limitless Achiever
k. The Optimist
l. The Intuitive

I named twelve Superpowers as archetypes to enhance your life experience. I interviewed everyday people to represent them because I wanted you to realize how accessible your Superpowers are. There are listed a few famous people who I believe own aspects of each Superpower.

As you read the following chapters about each Superpower, be attentive to identifying your strongest Superpower. Notice what words or examples call out to you. You may recall memories of using it for an outstanding outcome. Become aware when you see a Superpower active within your circle of friends, family or community. Recall historical figures that you admire and have displayed a Superpower on this list. We all access different ones for different intentions, and I believe *you* can access all twelve Superpowers in your lifetime.

Conscious Journaling

Before we delve into what each of these labels fully entails, take a moment to reflect on your interpretation of your Superpower. Listen to your first response. Write it down so you can see it. Share the results with someone who is a good listener or someone who could benefit from knowing you.

1. Now that you have discovered your Superpowers, where do they show up for you? At work? At home? In your community? In your relationships?

Chapter Summary

We all have a Superpower that is an inherent, stand out quality that we can access to achieve a particular outcome. It is important to know your Superpower(s) so you can consciously activate it daily in your life experiences. We can determine our dominant Superpower by evaluating our behaviors in different contexts. It is possible to actuate all twelve Superpowers in your lifetime.

Chapter 2

THE ACTIVATOR: CELEBRATE INSPIRED ACTION

"The path to success is to take massive determined action."
—Tony Robbins

Activators are open, honest, straightforward, and direct. They turn the emotional drive into physical action and avoid details that could slow them down. When they can rely on an ally to organize the details of their plan it propels them forward unfettered.

Activators move without fear because it could impede progress. Fearless risk-taking is part of their impetus. Uncertainty does not hinder them as they accept this is the exciting part of taking risks. When Activators motivate others, they do so with inspirational words, inflection, and body language.

Activators have no trouble pointing out the elephant in the room. Instead of evaluating their actions beforehand, they will remain more driven by the impulse to break through any resistance. This does not necessarily mean that Activators are rude; instead, they are more likely to have the courage to speak up about taboo topics.

Activators are leaders and motivators. In everyday life you see them as pioneers of social, conceptual, and ideological movements. Coaches, CEOs, fitness trainers, and authors are some examples of Activators. They stand out on their own. They have the ability to awaken people to tap into their own capacity to motivate themselves. Activators can draw out strengths and skills in their followers.

Activators feel compelled to be in motion. As a result, they have a knack of seeing what is blocking action. They do not like to be bridled by limitation, so part of their

Superpower is identifying limits so they can *break-through* them. Because they are willing to put themselves out there fearlessly, they tend to breakthrough limits and blocks efficiently. They are great mentors to enlist when you desire an experience you may have feared attempting previously.

Activators get inspired by goal setting and goal achieving. They are always aiming higher to perform their best and support others to do so also. This nourishes their Superpower.

As I reflected on the people in my world who might be Activators, I saw repeatedly how my yoga student, Sam, is an Activator in how he approaches his life, relationships and career. Sam is a father of 2 sons and he is dedicated to their health, happiness and success. He owns several successful businesses and invests in up-and-coming companies. He has traveled around the world, meeting exciting people wherever he goes. When I asked him how he saw himself as an Activator, he did not recognize having this Superpower because he never stopped to reflect on his Superpower. This epiphany (or lack thereof due to his constant movement) illustrates the Activator to a T.

Sam first remembered being an Activator as a student advisor and soccer team captain at a boarding school in Great Britain. He recalls the challenge of transforming novice, insecure individuals into members of a consistent, winning team. Sam didn't realize at the time, but he had eagerly stepped in as an Activator, encouraging the team to work together and triumph. As an advisor, struggling students approached him for help, and he could sense how they were holding themselves back. As usual, he took steps to re-kindle their confidence.

How does Sam access his Superpower now? He uses the same methods he used as an advisor and captain: he seeks out what is limiting people to their highest potential. Sam's Superpower is mostly accessed through his deliberate use of asking thoughtful questions. He is comfortable asking questions that may be taboo and may reveal someone's vulnerability. He finds that this can reveal someone's blind side and result in revealing their block. As a parent he engages with his sons in depth, about their happiness and what they want to achieve in life. He asks thought provoking questions so they have to pause and be introspective before offering an answer. Sam prefers they find their own answer but he wants to lead them into their self-examination with his style of questioning.

In addition, he is an Activator in leading employees to successful outcomes. In training his managers, he consults with those who are veering off track in performance. He identifies how they are not in alignment with their skills and strengths. Sam motivates them to realign with their end goal. Sam will reveal how fear may be hindering their progress. Additionally, Sam likes to cook big meals and throw big parties for his team members as a bonding activity. The shared experience cultivates good will and warm emotions for that helps the community mesh with each other.

What is crucial Sam's Superpower? He chooses to surround himself with happy, optimistic friends and staff who round out his talents. Sam prioritizes hydration, exercise, healthy food, and rest. Yoga and breathing practices are essential ingredients in his daily routine. Sam also encourages his employees to practice wellness habits, as their health supports his business growth.

Sam must have quiet, reflective time at the end of his day with reading or being in meditation. This helps him integrate ideas and formulate new questions for tomorrow.

What strategy does he use to hone his Superpower? Two catalysts motivate him to be an Activator: a passion for creating and a passion for helping others in need. Sam uses his love of cooking for others to stimulate ideas for his Superpower. He reads many genres of books, then mentally debates the pros and cons, remaining receptive to ideas for potential growth. In addition, he looks at an event, person, or relationship and evaluates the beauty in it. By syncing these thoughts with deep, relaxed breathing, he can exhale judgment and inhale acceptance.

What are the pitfalls to having this Superpower? Patience can be a challenge when Sam feels delayed from progress. Activators need to maintain healthy boundaries with work and down time, while simultaneously setting multiple objectives in motion. Constant activity can push him into a "body breakdown state" filled with exhaustion and pain. Activators may face the pitfall of dissatisfaction with the here and now, as they believe there is always another summit to reach.

How does Sam recharge? Gaining new perspectives from world travel always refuels his creativity and goal setting tendencies. Alternately, solitude is just as vital. He finds solace in reading books that challenge his thought process and introduce him to diverse mindsets. He relies on regular bodywork and massage to release tension and stress.

What blocks Sam's Superpower? He feels frustrated when people don't take immediate action from his advice. Sam loathes procrastination. He also dislikes feeling bridled by limiting thoughts or actions. When he feels dissatisfied by a slow process toward outcome, he switches his focus to his love of learning. Activators never block themselves, in his opinion. The nature of their Superpower is to progress forward.

Famous Activators: Michael Phelps, Queen Latifah and Tony Robbins.

***

Your Affirmation: "I move with passion and conviction."

Conscious Journaling

Take a moment to reflect on your interpretation of the Activator Superpower. Observe what people may have come to your mind as you read this passage. Journal from the prompts of the following questions. Listen to your first response to each and write it down so you can see it. Share the results with someone who is a good listener or someone who could benefit from knowing you better.

1. What qualities or actions do I have that resonate with the Activator Superpower?

2. Who do I know is an Activator and why?

3. What are some ways I could benefit from having an Activator mentor me?

Chapter Summary

The Activator is a Superpower to seek and cultivate when you need to take decisive action. They are motivate and lead with inspiring words and actions that hearten fearless risk taking. Activators make great coaches, CEOs, leaders, authors and motivational speakers.

Chapter 3

THE AMPLIFIER: CELEBRATE HAVING A VOLUME DIAL

> "The roots of all goodness lie in the soil of appreciation for goodness."
>
> —The Dalai Lama

The person with this Superpower is sensitive enough to feel the emotion of a person or environment *and* have the skills to influence that energy. Amplifiers can elevate energy with enthusiasm, emotion, inspiration and praise. Conversely, Amplifiers can use their Superpower to dissipate tension. I often identify Amplifiers in my world as the people that "light up a room" when they enter with just their "being." This is a powerful gift when used for elevating people's consciousness, mood and spirits. The intensity of this Superpower can work negatively if they become the proverbial "wet blanket" and dampen enthusiasm, darken an atmosphere with their gloomy disposition. Now those people are not *trying* to activate their Superpower in those moments, they are just being their Amplifier self.

How can they consciously access their Superpower with an audience or group? The Amplifier must tune into the intention for the gathering. They merge or "feel into" their subject (e.g. their audience, students, relationships)to deepen their understanding of them. Now they alter their language/words, behavior, emotions, and overall energy to match that intention. The Amplifiers lead with the resonating energy needed to match the desired journey and destination.

Think of comedians. They think of their goal: tune audience to sense of humor and laughter. They must know their audience. What might they be feeling that evening?

Where do they come from? What motivates them? Next they deliver relatable material with relatable words, inflections, timing and body language to *that* audience to lead them to their sense of humor and ultimately, laughter. The comedic Amplifier adjusts their delivery to the feedback that comes back from their audience. They see what brings a big laugh by what energy they put out there. Their Superpower is always informing them on how much of a "dose" of inflection, words, timing to achieve the laugh. This may be calculated in the preparation of a routine but more organic and intuitive when they are in the moment of a performance.

An Amplifier is what I call a "people person." Amplifiers are motivated by their desire to connect with people. They relish in engaging and learning with their world through relationships. Amplifiers are gifted with words, sentiment, and action. People are attracted to and respond to Amplifiers' assertions. By manipulating the emotional environment, they can provide and elevate encouragement when impetus is low. Think of them as a 'mood barometer' with an added volume dial to increase or decrease the energy depending on an environment. Although it sounds as though this Superpower is only useful for the benefit of others, however, the Amplifier benefits from the gratification they get from satisfying others; it recharges them.

Because Amplifiers have a natural tendency to make an environment feel a certain way, people tend to give them a spotlight. It is vital to Amplifiers that they are in alignment with the greater good for whom they are amplifying. When Amplifiers remain neutral to their internal feelings about the intention of the group, it helps them focus on the needs of the group. To illustrate this Superpower, I interviewed a choral conductor, John, a perfect example of an Amplifier.

John first recognized his Superpower when he was studying music in college. He watched successful conductors and noticed how their leadership inspired him. He observed how they created a cohesive ensemble and repeated what one of his mentors told him: "Copy from the best, leave the rest."

How does John access his Superpower now? He merges with the song on a mental and emotional level. He notes on the music when and where to elevate intensity or soften the mood to create his desired effect. John knows his singers inside and out. He spends the necessary amount of time to to communicate effectively with each member, each group within the chorus (e.g. Altos, Tenors, Sopranos, etc.) and the group as whole. His auditory senses guide him throughout rehearsals. John also follows his head and gut feelings to stay with the intention of each piece of music. He modifies his singers' voices in measured amounts. He chooses to serve the *process* of the rehearsal, not his own needs. Regularly checking in with his perceptions of the music and emotions, he maintains alignment with the song's energy and the ensemble of the choir.

What is crucial to his Superpower? Adequate rest, sleep, diet, and exercise. He is faithful to a Hatha yoga practice and enjoys being close to the earth by working in his vegetable garden. He also finds it essential to clear his ego before rehearsal. His mantra is: "I am here to serve them, not me." His sense of humor helps him from taking himself too seriously. When I asked him about his Superpower, John laughed and quoted the movie *Spinal Tap*, "Our amplifiers go to 11!"

What strategy does he use to hone his Superpower? In rehearsal, John is attentive, opening himself to the process, moment to moment. He places little post-it notes on his sheet music to stay on course, including phrases, such as: "lead them," "teach them," "guide them," and "love them." His principles that guide his Amplifier Superpower are partially inspired by two habits of his mentor, Westin Noble, from Luther College. Mr. Noble would walk across campus every morning to throw away litter to beautify the campus. At the end of his day he would write in a journal, chronicling what went well and what could be improved.

What are some pitfalls to being an Amplifier? Being more sensitive, John's version of this Superpower can take feedback and outcomes personally. No matter what happens in rehearsal, John will analyze and overthink the events until the following day. He mentally replays any perceived negative comments and carries it as a reflection of his flaws. This can get in his way of being in a positive mindset and seeing how his Superpower enabled the rehearsal.

How does John recharge his Superpower? To unwind from rehearsal, he likes to relax and meditate with a cup of tea in his garden. On his days off, he observes respected colleagues. He reads motivational books, like *The Great Work of Your Life* by Stephen Cope and *Do You Quantum Think?* by Dianne Collins. He also gets regular massages to release stress and tension from his body.

THE AMPLIFIER: CELEBRATE HAVING A VOLUME DIAL • 27

What blocks his Superpower? Overthinking can get in his way of living in the moment. If John is unable to be completely present and dwells on a disappointing past event, it can inhibit his ability to tune into the current needs of his audience or group.

Famous Amplifiers: His Holiness Dalai Lama, Stevie Wonder, Mary Oliver, Rumi.

***

Your Affirmation: I elevate my experience with enthusiasm and passion.

Conscious Journaling

Take a moment to reflect on your interpretation of the Amplifier Superpower. Observe what people may have come to your mind as you read this passage. Journal from the prompts of the following questions. Listen to your first response to each and write it down so you can see it. Share the results with someone who is a good listener or someone who could benefit from knowing you better.

1. What qualities or actions do I have that resonate with the Amplifier Superpower?

2. Who do I know is an Amplifier and why?

3. What are some ways I could benefit from having an Amplifier mentor me?

Chapter Summary

If the volume of energy, emotion or inspiration needs boosting, it's time to call the Amplifier. They have a knack of tuning into others and modifying their words, actions and emotions to heighten inspiration or create tranquility. They use their sensitivity and adaptability to match intentions in relationships with desired journeys and outcomes. They make great comedians, conductors, motivational speakers, actors and models.

Chapter 4

THE OBSERVER: CELEBRATE THE BIG PICTURE

"The day is coming when a single carrot, freshly observed, will set off a revolution."

—Paul Cezanne

Observers can blend into the background to gather information by observing details *and* seeing the grand scheme of things. Observers are people watchers. They are driven by intense curiosity of people, animals, environments. They want to understand people's motivations, beliefs and actions. Active listening is important skill to being an Observer. This is revealed to them in watching their subject's speech, inflection, and body language.

Another important aspect of being an Observer is their need to share their gathered information. They have a gift of offering perspective with observations and they need to feel safe from judgement in sharing their observations. They could be somewhat tentative in sharing their reflections with an unfamiliar group, especially if they do not sense their information will be understood and valued.

Observers are also well-practiced in neutrality. By detaching themselves emotionally from the subject of their observations, they can assess an approach and an outcome from an unbiased vantage point. Observers benefit from having a journal, voice memo, or blog to hold all of the accumulated information.

We can access this Superpower in many roles. As parents we can observer our children's behavior to inform us of their needs and how to guide them. Being an

Observer can inform a broad spectrum of careers because it adds valuable information about the big picture objectives as well as revealing details that could be overlooked. Poets, authors and filmmakers as Observers reveal a perspective of a character's motivations and stance in the story. Medical professionals and attorneys can benefit from the neutral vantage point of the Observer to better serve their patients and clients.

Why is it important to have a big picture perspective when we are focusing on creating a desired experience and/or outcome? We often can get myopic in our zeal to get "there" to the goal. When we get short-sighted we might miss crucial details that could guide us to important modifications in our approach. This can often save time, money, wasted efforts. When I was writing this book I would get caught up with completion deadlines I had set for myself. I would push myself to complete a certain number of chapters by a date without factoring time to process *what* I wrote. In doing so I lost sight of what was most important: providing my readers with a powerful guidebook to gain insight on their Superpowers. Once I began meeting with my book buddy, Mary-Lou, she became my Observer, offering neutral perspective on how to make my book better.

To illustrate this Superpower, I interviewed my friend, Claudia, a lifelong fabric and textile artist. She is devoted to her family, art, reading, journaling and studying French language and culture.

Claudia has been aware of her Observer Superpower all of her life. As a young child, she was shy, preferring to spend time alone. At home with her three brothers, or at school with her classmates, she always liked to watch rather than participate.

How does she activate her Superpower now? Claudia enjoys observing in social, travel, and artistic settings. She sees herself as unbiased, listening to many sides of a story without falling into a black-or-white mindset. Even though being an Observer serves others, she does not always share her observations. She will hold back her Superpower if she senses it may hinder someone's expression of creativity. She wants to help with her observation and avoid superimposing an idea to influence a friend, family member or colleague. Claudia wants her observations to be perceived impartial perceptions not judgments.

What is crucial to her Superpower? It is fundamental for her to log her insights into a journal. She likes to handwrite on paper *and* keep some of her reflections in a laptop.

Equally important is for Claudia to remain unbiased. As a participant in art guilds, Claudia observes, sits with her notes for a period of time, then offers feedback to the group. Having time for reflection of her observations is also crucial to gain insights on the overall view. She often journals about how to share her insights to each audience she observes so they can hear her broad view.

What strategy does she use to hone her observation skills? Quiet reflection helps her fit together all the pieces of information. Nature is the perfect environment for quiet moments, and she journals to help organize her thoughts. In a group, Claudia feels it is essential to use her Superpower as a positive contribution. Self-confidence determines her choice to reveal information, so Claudia tries to establish rapport with a person or group. She provides unbiased insights, which engage discussion and ease decision making.

How does she recharge her Superpower? Traveling and people-watching is her main go-to that nourishes Claudia's Superpower. She can wander museums, libraries and galleries observing people and artwork. Her love of learning always renews her. When retreating with her family, friends or quilt group she often plays different word and math games to keep her mind sharp. She enjoys spending time with her children and grandchildren, observing the knowledge that spans the different generations. Her avid reading books and studying French replenishes her desire for knowledge. Attending quilting retreats, art exhibits, and political forums also expands her thinking. Being in a book club is fun because she gets to hear others' perspectives.

What are some pitfalls of being an Observer? Claudia admits she often gets caught up in observing rather than doing, which may lead to procrastination. To address this tendency, Claudia keeps a list of to do's for the day and week.

What can block her Superpower? When circumstances prevent her from sharing observations, she feels overwhelmed. Claudia recalls a trip to London where she happily devoted five days to museums and bookshops. After being solo for so long, her observations overwhelmed her. She needed someone to listen to and value her observations. An additional block to her Superpower is her sensitivity to others' reactions to her feedback. It can restrict her from sharing and she may withhold reflections due to fear of judgment. Because of this fear, she may need more time to strategize how to reveal observations before divulging them.

Famous Observers: Georgia O'Keefe, Jane Goodall, Jacques Cousteau

Your Affirmation: I observe with curiosity and neutrality.

Conscious Journaling

Take a moment to reflect on your interpretation of the Observer Superpower. Observe what people may have come to your mind as you read this passage. Journal from the prompts of the following questions. Listen to your first response to each and write it down so you can see it. Share the results with someone who is a good listener or someone who could benefit from knowing you better.

1. What qualities or actions do I have that resonate with the Observer Superpower?

2. Who do I know is an Observer and why?

3. What are some ways I could benefit from having an Observer mentor me?

Chapter Summary

Observers are powerful allies because they bear witness to valuable elements of our experience. Their neutrality can reveal grander perspectives for growth and expansion. Observers need time to observe, reflect, and trust before revealing their findings. When we take time to receive the reflections of an Observer it can guide us on how to modify our approach to cultivate a gratifying journey at a satisfying destination. Observers are great artists, writers, poets, leaders, and activists.

Chapter 5

THE TRANSFORMER: CELEBRATE METAMORPHOSIS

"Transformation literally means going beyond your form."

—Wayne Dyer

People with this Superpower get fired up by change. They know how to motivate, inspire, and open pathways for evolution. They are great with transitions because they see the ingredients needed to implement positive change.

Transformers are "game-changers." Revolution equals adventure to a Transformer. They lift us up out of humdrum apathy with inspirational wisdom, vision and excitement. They model what drives them. They meet resistance with conscious awareness, never shying from a challenge. They are great with envisioning possibilities, planning for them then executing them. I see most Transformers have an early aptitude for embracing change then expand their Superpower over time.

Transformers are drawn to feel fluid and dynamic in their life. Stagnation can trigger their awareness that something 'doesn't feel quite right." That awareness gets their juices flowing with ideas for change. They know change can reset and rejuvenate one's approach to life challenges.

Being highly inventive individuals, they are fueled by passionate creativity. Routine may be challenging for Transformers as they feel most alive when things are new and different.

Another benefit of this Superpower is that they can be grounded and be in-motion. Grounding into the present moment helps them intuit what needs to change right now. Intuition informs the Transformer of the next step necessary to advance the changeover.

An experienced Transformer understands that fear and risk taking is part of metamorphosis. A seasoned Transformer will step INTO fear with both feet. They see the steps needed OUTSIDE of the comfort zone and go there willingly. Therefore Transformers are great mentors to support evolution with people who prefer certainty and predictability. Their skill is to observe the resistance and sense what dose of inspiration is needed to breakthrough fears.

Fitness trainers make excellent Transformers as they guide clients to develop their minds and bodies. They have to keep a pulse on fitness and diet trends to keep their clients committed to their programs. This propels them to switch up routines and diet recommendations to keep their clients engaged with enthusiasm. Transformers are catalysts driven by a need to keep life experiences fresh and inviting.

Lisa, a Transformer who has a private practice in life coaching, mentored me through a much needed transformation. I came to her for help reframing how to run my business. I was in pain from overworking. She taught me productive ways to change my business that ultimately showed me how to "work smarter not harder." She helped me to convert my schedule and business practices that prioritized my health first. It cultivated a new mindset and energy for my business that enabled a better version of me. As I incorporated her suggestions I began to feel a renewed sense of vitality. This shows how Transformers not only change physical situations but they revise mindsets and approaches by tuning into alternative possibilities.

Lisa recalls always being comfortable with change. Late in her teens and into college, she realized change was easy for her.

How does she access her Superpower now? Lisa has created her business around her Superpower. She remains present to her clients' needs and receives guidance from her intuition. She gifts them with tools, clarity, and intention to rework their lives. When Lisa is leading a workshop, speaking publicly, or working with a client, her entire focus is on gathering energy to foster change. She does this by listening and offering a vision of possibility that goes beyond current limitations. She believes we transform by moving beyond old patterns. Once we believe new possibilities exist, we can realign with life-changing perspectives, ideas, and action.

What is crucial to her Superpower? While Lisa appreciates continuity and structure, she is acutely aware of the necessity to refresh her surroundings. She easily rearranges the furniture in her house or office, and does not feel a need to have an overly familiar routine. She also needs to stay balanced with exercise, healthy diet and time for meditation and journaling. These habits keep her on target with accessing her Superpower. Another crucial element to her Superpower that has grown over time is patience. She can't rush an insight or metamorphosis in herself or others. There is an element of trust can comes in with patience. Trust allows one to be in stages of transformation until they are complete to move on to the next.

What is her strategy to sharpen her Superpower? Lisa meditates with what is happening now to get a feel for what needs to change. She then visualizes different possible outcomes. She often uses the phrase, "What will it feel like if…," and daydreams about limitless, potential pathways and destinations. If she is learning something new, she allows herself to inhabit the mindset of a beginner. This opens her to receive new information. She needs to be relaxed, present, and comfortable to integrate new material.

How does she recharge her Superpower? Attending women's workshops and retreats with like minded practitioners can give her ideas and replenish her ambition. Doing yoga and meditation solitary or with a group also nourishes Lisa. She will take time out to do thermal hydrotherapy when she needs to renew her physical body especially after moving through an especially draining transition. Her love of learning compels her to read motivational books about change and healing. It helps her reformulate new perspectives on varying approaches. From time to time she also recharges her Superpower by being mentored by a life or business coach who can be the Transfomer for her. By receiving transformational guidance and support, it gives her a client's perspective.

What are some pitfalls to being a Transformer? Lisa is challenged by mundane, daily repetition. Regular routines can be tedious and boring for her. Conversely, she finds herself reaching to create the next event rather than living in the moment. Only with age and wisdom has she has learned to slow down her impulse to change and appreciate the blessings of the moment.

What blocks her Superpower? A lack of clarity of what needs to transform can block her. This can happen if she is too close or attached to a journey or outcome. When she is unclear of how to modify her mindset or approach, she places herself in nature. Hiking or walking along the beach grounds her, quieting her mind. Repeated meditation and breathing let her see the next crucial step for the most beneficial outcome. She will journal for a period of time about something that feels incongruent with where she needs to be or feel.

Lisa also grapples with using her Superpower at home. When she is closer to a person, the more challenging it is for her to remain neutral to reading what change would benefit them. Her Superpower works best when she is open to the outcome. Stepping back from a situation enables her to ask relevant questions, resets her energy and offer perspective that may help modify the experience.

Famous Transformers: Mahatma Gandhi, Maya Angelou, Martin Luther King, jr.

***

Your Affirmation: I allow myself to change with flow and ease.

Conscious Journaling

Take a moment to reflect on your interpretation of the Transformer Superpower. Observe what people may have come to your mind as you read this passage. Journal from the prompts of the following questions. Listen to your first response to each and write it down so you can see it. Share the results with someone who is a good listener or someone who could benefit from knowing you better.

38 • THE SUPERPOWER PLAYBOOK

1. What qualities or actions do I have that resonate with the Transformer Superpower?

2. Who do I know is a Transformer and why?

3. What are some ways I could benefit from having an Transformer mentor me?

Chapter Summary

Transformers help us accept change and find prosperous ways of adapting. They show us how life is a series of stages toward overall improvement. With the Transformer's fluid nature, we see how releasing fear of change makes more possibilities accessible. Trust and patience are crucial elements in tuning into our Superpower of Transformation. Transformers make great mentors, health practitioners, dieticians, thought leaders and teachers.

Chapter 6

THE INNOVATOR: CELEBRATE MODIFICATION

"Never doubt that a small group of thoughtful, committed citizens can change the world; indeed, it's the only thing that ever has."

—Margaret Mead

Innovators modify concepts to improve them. They have the neutrality of the Observer combined with the curiosity about the inner workings of an idea. This drives the Innovator toward creating solutions to problems. Problem-solving energizes them to take ideas to the next level of being. They do not feel stymied by unexpected outcomes, instead this compels them to dive deeper into their process of taking apart each step of the approach to the problem. By breaking each step down, they can revise some aspect of it, then observe the results. These aspects of the Innovator reveal their core virtues of patience and trust. They have this immense capacity to suspend any attachment to specific results. This aligns their Superpower to ensure the path to getting to the solution is going to align with the current reality.

I have a client who is a corporate project manager of software engineers. She sets out timelines for the project and progressional steps to reach completion deadlines. As Innovator, she knows the skillset of each engineer and when to ask them to tweak their approach when progress hits a wall. She changes her leadership and support style to accommodate where they are in the process throughout the project, to meet the demands of the present moment. Although she is not an engineer, her Innovator Superpower guides her to speak their language adapting her words so they can understand and receive her guidance.

Innovators have internal focus keeps them on track without needing any external motivation. They are passionate about changing approaches and accept that there can be varying outcomes to developing a new concept, invention, or pathway.

Innovators may have a tendency to get lost in tinkering with a project because of their tenacious nature and may lose track of time. When they are "onto something" it can seem obsessive. They embrace patience within the discovery process and prefer taking risks. Sometimes they create new things by repurposing parts or ideas. A spontaneous Innovator can make impromptu choices with spontaneous brainstorming. Having their flexibility releases limitations and opens them up to tapping into expansive potentials.

Innovators can operate in any realm. We often see them inventing products, software, techniques, movements and mindsets. This is due to their ability to hone in on what needs to adapt. They resonate that information with their approach toward creation and solution. Trial and error informs them on how to modify skills needed on the journey.

When I asked Cynthia, a teacher from Alaska, if I could her interview her as the Innovator, she deflected the notion. She thought the title belonged to her brother, a mechanical engineer. I convinced her that there are many types of Innovators. We can be innovators of ideas in any application.

Her first experience of being exposed to an Innovator teacher was when Cynthia was in a multi-level, multi-age classroom for Asian studies in a Berkeley middle school. She learned as a student to value different pathways of learning. Her experience with this teacher influenced her to become an Innovator.

How does she access her Superpower now? By working in unique learning environments. For example, she recently wrote a grant to help produce a student-filmed documentary about local Valdez history. Students practiced interviewing skills while recording stories from "Old town" Valdez Residents. She made their learning experiential and memorable outside of a traditional classroom. As a LEGO Robotics coach, she asked engaging questions, helping her students develop real-world solutions to problems like recycling plastic trash. She now works with kindergarteners and creates new ways to set up the classroom for each skill set they are mastering. Cynthia looks for current themes in their environment to reshape into learning opportunities.

Living and parenting her sons in Alaska—utilizing unique resources to meet family needs—requires an innovative mindset as well. She has learned to adapt with the changing climate and the sometimes harsh conditions of Alaska.

What is crucial to her Superpower? Fulfilling needs that stretch her limits invigorate her Superpower. Happy students and families amplify her Superpower. Additionally, Cynthia requires daily exercise and journaling. She surrounds herself with intriguing colleagues who share ideas and act as a sounding board keep her uplifted. Another crucial natural element for her is water therapies and swimming. Water pulls her out of her head and offers insights she may not have originally considered.

What is her strategy to hone her Superpower? She writes lists of pros and cons then analyzes what is working and what is in conflict. She seeks TED talks, edutopia.org, and NPR to offer alternative perspectives on pertinent subject matters. Cynthia will often use online archives of prior methods to see how they worked in particular contexts. She aligns her intention with a desired outcome and remains open to altering her approach if she sees things are not working toward her initial objective.

How does she recharge her Superpower? Cynthia attends educational programs in Anchorage. She reads related books and listens to podcasts. Cynthia finds inspiration in books like *Teach Like Your Hair is on Fire* by Rafe Esquith and *Teach Like a Pirate* by Dave Burgess. Running is her daily recharge to release stress and pent-up energy.

What are the pitfalls of being an Innovator? She feels unsatisfied when she thinks she can do more. This self-critical mindset leads her to compare herself with other innovators and focus on where she thinks she falls short. To address this pitfall, she follows a strategy learned from a keynote address by Lee Watanabe Crockett of Global Digital Citizen Foundation (https://globaldigitalcitizen.org/) called "The Committed Sardine." The metaphor encourages one to look for a few sardines that create a new movement in an entirely different direction. It is a method of searching for fellow Innovators and uniting with them, forging a new movement. Another pitfall for her can be follow-through; she has so many ideas pouring into her that she can feel scattered at times, leading to a feeling overwhelm.

What blocks her Superpower? Cynthia often feels blocked by two mindsets: those resisting positive change and those who make excuses about why things cannot ever change. These mindsets only impede progress toward positive change and they have the capacity to shut her down.

Famous Innovators: Alton Brown, Marianne Williamson, Elon Musk

***

Your Affirmation: I pioneer new ideas to create new pathways to success.

Conscious Journaling

Take a moment to reflect on your interpretation of the Innovator Superpower. Observe what people may have come to your mind as you read this passage. Journal from the prompts of the following questions. Listen to your first response to each and write it down so you can see it. Share the results with someone who is a good listener or someone who could benefit from knowing you better.

1. What qualities or actions do I have that resonate with the Innovator Superpower?

2. Who do I know who is an Innovator and why?

   [ ]

3. What are some ways I could benefit from having an Innovator mentor me?

   [ ]

Chapter Summary

Innovators are deep thinkers driven to improve life. They inspire us to think differently about everyday experiences to enhance them. It is a Superpower we can tap into to modify new versions of experiences. Innovators are great teachers, chefs, inventors, managers, investors, artists and editors.

CHAPTER 7

THE EXPANDER: CELEBRATE STRETCHING BEYOND LIMITS

"Imagination is more important than knowledge. For knowledge is limited, whereas imagination embraces the entire world, stimulating progress, giving birth to evolution."

—Albert Einstein

Expanders tap into far-reaching realms of possibilities. They are information gatherers with the capacity to think beyond what is known. They think "something more could possibly exist." Elaborating details comes second nature to them. Expanders can produce offshoots of an original idea. Their challenge lies in winnowing down.

Expanders have the skill to see the limitation in a concept. It lights them up because it compels their creativity. Creativity is at the forefront of this Superpower. Whereas some people find limitation as a pain point or frustration it acts as the "chocolate" dangling in front of an Expander making them drool. They embrace how the limit stimulates their vast imagination.

This is a Superpower to call on when you feel your shine has dulled and another one of your Superpower(s) have plateaued. The Expander helps us imagine other ways of being that may be outside our comfort zone. We often can get lulled into familiar routines of thinking that keep us confined by our attachment to certainty. This can shorten our range of expression of our Superpower(s) and keeps us playing small when we could be accessing our full range of expression. It is one small step outside your comfort zone where many enriching experiences are waiting for you. Chapter 14: Managing Fear offers Superpower strategies on how to move beyond fears that keep us hemmed in our comfort zone cage.

Expanders are broad thinkers. Seek an Expander when generating an idea for a new project, product or modality. They can sense what drawbacks exist in that concept that may hinder the full blown expression of that idea. Expanders are broad thinkers that tend to go beyond their first thought and idea.

I chose Donna, a graphic designer and product inventor, to exemplify an Expander. Donna has always been creative. In her family unit her father and artistic siblings motivated each other to consider options beyond their first idea. She recalls her father posing the open-ended question to them, "What if you try…?" This query encouraged his children to shift, opening up their current mindset. He also urged them to envision many pathways to what they wanted to achieve. Her father loved to repurpose items into new creations. I was in a women's business networking group when I met Donna. In meetings she was always jotting down notes and sharing her creative insights with our colleagues. She created a monthly lunch meetings to focus on troubleshooting business problems. The group would mastermind together to expand possible solutions.

How does Donna activate her Superpower now? Donna uses it in her approach to initial concepts that she has for inventions. She will journal about an original idea then list possibilities of many renditions of that original concept. At her job as an editorial assistant for a government agency, academic professors often walk into her office unsure how to format and present their concepts at symposiums. Donna goes beyond her role as "editorial assistant" and creates options for creative expression that they had not previously considered. Many people think of Donna as the "option queen."

What is crucial for her to be an Expander? Helping people find solutions to their challenges stimulates her Superpower. She considers work more like playtime because tweaking ideas bring her joy. Another important element to her Superpower is to end her day with gratitude for her blessings. Her imagination requires keeping an open mind and "drama-free zone." Donna always travels with journals, pens, and her phone to record voice memos. She also keeps a pen and paper next to her bed to jot down ideas that pop up in her dreams. She is emphatic about lists, and the adage, "write it down and make it happen," is a mantra for her. Alternatively, Donna needs quiet downtime. Being with like-minded, creative people adds volume to Donna's Superpower. Her compulsion to solve problems stimulates her imagination.

What is her strategy for her Superpower? Her main strategy for her Superpower is to write and log insights. Before cell phones she used to call her house and leave her ideas on her answering machine. She is involved in a writing group that keeps her accountable to finish her books and stories. Gazing at the ocean and other novel ways of changing her visual field, often stimulate her expansive vision. Her New Year's ritual of collaging inspirational pictures and words in a journal helps her theme her year. She reads books like *How to Think like Leonardo* by Michael Gelb and *Learn to Power Think* by Catarina Rando, which offer her boundless insights.

How does she recharge her Superpower? A short drive by the ocean allows her to regain clarity. When she finds herself over-thinking, she jumps in the shower. Being immersed in water often brings her an epiphany. Laying down and doing nothing can be productive because it allows her creativity to take a break. When she arises, she feels a renewed sense of openness. Donna also finds that doing mindless chores like sweeping the floor give her permission to take a break from creative thinking.

What are some pitfalls of being an Expander? She struggles to accept things as they are because she can always see ways to make improvements. Additionally, Donna continually gets enticed with the next idea before the last three or four have come to fruition. She revealed that her closet contains many journals packed with ideas for inventions and books. Donna would love to have a product development team to take her journals and develop her ideas into market ready products for distribution.

What blocks her Superpower? People and mindsets that are fixed, limited, and cynical repel her. She decided when she turned 50 she would no longer hang out with people she deemed "drains, strains, and pains." Any scarcity mentality is especially distasteful to her. When Donna feels blocked, she engages in a mundane activity, like doing the dishes, to clear her mind. Or, she goes on a long ride on the back of her husband's motorcycle to delve into her imagination. When an idea dawns on her, she asks him to pull over so she can write it down. (I imagine a lot of patience is required when traveling by motorcycle with Donna.

Famous Expanders: Dr. Masuru Emoto, Leonardo DaVinci, George Lucas

***

Your Affirmation: I expand my comfort zone to experience more from life.

Conscious Journaling

Take a moment to reflect on your interpretation of the Expander Superpower. Observe what people may have come to your mind as you read this passage. Journal from the prompts of the following questions. Listen to your first response to each and write it down so you can see it. Share the results with someone who is a good listener or someone who could benefit from knowing you better.

1. What qualities or actions do I have that resonate with the Expander Superpower?

2. Who do I know is an Expander and why?

3. What are some ways I could benefit from having an Expander mentor me?

Chapter Summary

Expanders can add a richness to our life by offering us ample options to express our ideas. By releasing limiting thoughts we may open ourselves to flourish in ways not previously that exist outside our comfort zone. Expanders are great visionaries, inventors, artists, authors, and scientists.

Chapter 8

THE CONTAINER: CELEBRATE SYSTEMS

"Having a clear mind and a clear space allows you to think and act with purpose."

—Erika Oppenheimer

The function of the Container is to "hold space." A Container knows how to hold individuals and groups accountable to their stated intention. They point out what may be out of alignment or outdated in a system. They have finesse with order and organization.

They are often skilled at making templates for events by providing a set of action steps to accomplish the goal of the event. An aspect of the Container's purpose is to generate clarity through order. This goes hand in hand with their ability to create the systems that maintain order. This Superpower can be expressed in varying renditions.

People with this Superpower know how to maintain the intention of an environment for a specific intention. Containers make excellent therapists because they understand how to "hold the space" for emotional expression while keeping everyone focused on healing. For example, a psychotherapist can keep a support group grounded and feeling validated so the members feel safe releasing painful emotions. They can "contain" the group if the members start veering off the trajectory of their healing intention.

People with this Superpower can be skilled leaders and healthcare practitioners. It is important that a Container remain open to change if the set course no longer serves the original intention. If they get too attached to their method this may limit growth. Flexibility serves Containers so they can remain open to modification. On a personal level, Containers are able to stick to a schedule and remain compliant with exercise, diet, and hygiene routines. Keeping themselves accountable to their health is part of their makeup.

Containers value time and punctuality. They value being dependable and reliable. Their promptness shows others that they value their time. Their respect for time shows their tenacity to being efficient and orderly.

I interviewed a friend, Cecile, who exemplifies a Container in all aspects of her life. Friends often call her to help them organize their closets, homes, and finances. She is an expert at clearing the clutter. She is also a proficient bookkeeper and tax accountant.

Cecile always regarded her Superpower as part of her nature when she was a young adult. Around 16 years old, she became truly aware that her actions created specific outcomes and felt inclined to create order and systems to keep herself accountable to her goals.

How does she access being a Container now? Cecile approaches every task with her Superpower. She looks at the desired outcome, then takes measured steps to make it happen. Organizing task lists, materials, and a timetables are fundamental. If she is creating a system whether bookkeeping or organizational, Cecile thinks about how that person's skillset can adhere to the system she invents for them.

What is crucial to her Superpower? Having daily lists, planners, and home organization are indispensable for her. Staying on target with diet, rest, and exercise are top priorities. Despite this need for structure, she likes to stay flexible about potential outcomes. Her sense of humor and non judgmental attitude soften her need for regiment.

What is her strategy to activate her Superpower? She makes a plan to match her desired intention, makes a list of essential elements, then executes her plan. Experience, time, and age have served Cecile as she consistently revises her approach to best serve herself and others. When starting a project with someone, she looks at their capacity to maintain the proposed system then makes shifts in the system that help the person adhere to the plan of action. Additionally, parenting a growing, changing child has taught her how to adapt her schedules and routines and still maintain a degree of order.

What are the pitfalls of being a Container? Cecile worries that others see her as controlling and over-opinionated. As a result, she rarely volunteers for a group of unfamiliar people. When people react negatively to her Superpower she tends to pull inward and hesitate to reach out even if she senses they could benefit from her Superpower.

How does Cecile recharge her Superpower? She loves to quiet her mind by working her garden. Cecile allows herself to take a weekend where she does nothing but catches up on movies or television shows. Being social with friends, enjoying nature, or just relaxing on her family's land in Napa renews her spirit. Reading books and magazines help her unwind after a long day.

What blocks her Container Superpower? When people resist changing old habits and beliefs that clearly do not serve them. Their limiting mindsets block their ability to be organized and hold a clean, uncluttered space. She witnessed this in past clients and friends whom she has set up organized systems. They tell themselves they can "never be organized" and they fulfill this prophecy. She acknowledges the power of attachment to limited thinking sabotages progress. Cecile feels *she* cannot block her Superpower—it perseveres in all situations.

Famous Containers: B.K.S. Iyengar, Martha Stewart, Marie Kondo

***

Your Affirmation: I create systems to access information and tools easily.

Conscious Journaling

Take a moment to reflect on your interpretation of the Container Superpower. Observe what people may have come to your mind as you read this passage. Journal from the prompts of the following questions. Listen to your first response to each and write it down so you can see it. Share the results with someone who is a good listener or someone who could benefit from knowing you better.

1. What qualities or actions do I have that resonate with the Container Superpower?

2. Who do I know is a Container and why?

3. What are some ways I could benefit from having a Container mentor me?

Chapter Summary

Through the lens of the Container, we see the benefit of creating organized systems to heighten clarity in our life. There are many versions of the Container as its function is to hold space for a desired intention. We can relax when the space around us feels uncluttered. Containers make great therapists, accountants, bookkeepers, and fitness trainers.

Chapter 9

THE SYNTHESIZER: CELEBRATE HARMONY

"I kept looking for a logic that would explain life. It never occurred to me that instead LOVE is the vital synthesis."

—Jane Roberts

Synthesizers are the glue in relationships and groups. They are motivated by the desire to feel harmonious with their inner and outer environments. These peacekeepers facilitate balance with their tranquil presence and their kindness.

Because of their desire to maintain unity, this Superpower bristles at the hint of conflict. Therefore, they are adept at identifying the thorn in relationships. They have the gift of a unique type of empathy that hones in on conflict so as to diffuse it with lightness and softness. Synthesizers are driven to to feel comfortable in their own body in addition to pleasing others. Their ultimate driving force is to end suffering. They draw from a well of compassion that drives their empathy. Understanding and implementing what is necessary to release tension is their primary objective. Love is their guiding principle--reminding us about what is most important in living a quality existence.

Because they are easy going and well liked, they may belong to different circles. In fact, a Synthesizer can fit in with most any faction of people because they relate to people through acceptance and avoid judgement. Superficiality repels this Superpower as does big egos.

One asset of this Superpower is that they have the ability connect people who may benefit one another. They can remember some aspect about a person and connect them to another who may be of service. This shows how Synthesizers make great networkers because they can sense like-minded people and hook them up. Because of their quest for harmony, Synthesizers have a good instinct about how people will meld and predict how their gifts will work together. Facilitating community is their forte because they have a strong sense of how people's assets will blend. Synthesizers love to generate community.

Synthesizers love community and give of themselves generously to improve their community. Volunteering is second nature to them. They use their good natured disposition to motivate others to do the same. They are a great Superpower to call on to be public service providers and leaders of nonprofit organizations.

I immediately saw the Synthesizer Superpower in one of my yoga students, Rob. When he joined my long established yoga class of women, Rob gracefully transitioned into this tight knit group with his easygoing nature. His gentle nature instantly warmed up the class. There are never any awkward moments when Rob is around because he acts as a buffer for any tension. His calmness and sense of humor always lightens the environment. He shared his eagerness to make people laugh. Rob has always used humor to get along with most people since early childhood.

How does he activate his Superpower now? To enable his Superpower, he has to feel relaxed in his skin. In order to do this, he tunes into the tension and what would release that tension. Rob is a seasoned bluegrass musician who plays with professional bands and he uses his Superpower to facilitate cohesion within the group rehearsals. He senses when the mood is sour and shifts the energy by making people laugh.

What is crucial to his Superpower? He needs the balance. He prefers a blend of masculine and feminine energy in his relationships. He needs equal time of social engagement and restorative solitude. Being in community is essential for his emotional well being. He has a flair for tuning into the reality of a present moment and shifting the emotional current to create balance. In music, he naturally intuits how the band needs to be situated to bring out the soul of the song. Another crucial ingredient to his Superpower is adaptability. A Synthesizer needs to be able to adjust to the changing feelings in the environment. He finds that being around people amplifies his Superpower. Yoga classes allow him to connect to others while re-aligning himself internally with his spirituality.

What tools does he use to hone his Superpower? Rob uses his affinity for symmetry to guide his musical expertise when leading rehearsals. If he senses people hemming and hawing about a direction, he will choose to lead the group with decisive direction. In social contexts, his intuition and empathy empower him to cultivate peaceful communication. Growing up with three sisters taught him how to own and express his emotions. His deep sense of gratitude for life enhances his Superpower.

What are some pitfalls of his Superpower? Maintaining compassion can be problematic if he takes feedback too personally. Frustration with divisive political opinions can disintegrate his compassion for himself and others. Another pitfall is when he feels out of balance or depressed he can tend to isolate himself from others which only exacerbates the imbalance.

How does Rob recharge his Superpower? Going to a local coffee shop and socializing with locals or playing music at nursing homes and hospice centers can really invigorate Rob's Superpower. Yoga and meditation bring him back to balance. To revive his inspiration, he seeks out nature, especially feeling renewed by backpacking and hiking in the mountains. Gardening resets his mind. Doing housework helps him release tension. Being around older people and babies can make him more aware of what is truly essential in life. They pull him out of patterns of overthinking and tune him into the present moment.

What blocks his Superpower? When he feels he can't access his sense of humor, he feels stymied. States of disharmony and war in the world can really make Rob feel out of sorts. He feels the discord of the world empathically. Narcissistic people are the nemesis to his Superpower. He avoids engaging with people who are not selfless in their nature.

Famous Synthesizers: Pam Grout, Jack Johnson, Eckhart Tolle.

***

Your Affirmation: I cultivate harmony through acceptance.

Conscious Journaling

Take a moment to reflect on your interpretation of the Synthesizer Superpower. Observe what people may have come to your mind as you read this passage. Journal from the prompts of the following questions. Listen to your first response to each and write it down so you can see it. Share the results with someone who is a good listener or someone who could benefit from knowing you better.

1. What qualities or actions do I have that resonate with the Synthesizer Superpower?

2. Who do I know is a Synthesizer and why?

3. What are some ways I could benefit from having a Synthesizer mentor me?

Chapter Summary

The Synthesizer naturally prefers connection and equilibrium in relationships. By acknowledging what makes them feel balanced and what creates discord, Synthesizers can decipher how to cultivate peace in groups. Synthesizers are adept at creating community in the world. Synthesizers make great musicians, marketing consultants, public relations consultants, non profit volunteers, interpreters, mediators, and teachers.

CHAPTER 10

THE EMPATH: CELEBRATE WALKING IN ANOTHER'S SHOES

"Empathy is about standing in someone else's shoes and feeling his/her heart, seeing with his/her eyes. Not only is Empathy hard to outsource or automate, but it makes the world a better place."
—Daniel H. Pink

People with this Superpower merge with others' pain, emotions, and feelings. They can feel other people's emotions as if they are their own. I often meet clients who are highly sensitive empaths and they find the world unbearably overwhelming. In my classes at my "Spiritual Detective Academy," I train students to visualize small "energy filters," placed in front of their belly so as to drain other people's energy they may have unconsciously absorbed. This mental tool helps them to separate others' emotional energy from their own. Once they have that clarity they can take deeper levels of ownership of their personal feelings and give others the responsibility to feel theirs. This provides them a greater awareness of how they may have been taking on more than their share of emotional burdens and stress.

Empathy may have developed from a sense of urgency from abusive childhood experiences. From my Intuitive energy coaching experiences, I have worked with many addicts who came from abusive family backdrops. From early childhood, they used their ability to feel energy and emotion in an environment so they would know if they were safe, needed to hide, or buffer the tension with their behavior in some way.

Unfortunately when these unhealthy conditions formulate a Superpower, it is not grown with core virtues like trust, love and gratitude. It is grown from a sense of fear and survival.

When Empaths are nurtured in a loving community of acceptance their Superpower enhances the community and relationships with their perspective. This is one of the most valuable assets of the Empath. Their ability to offer emotional context aids those who are less attuned to understanding emotions of others. It is important for those people to align with an Empath to reveal other viewpoints and foster compassionate understanding in a community.

It is important for an Empath to feel safe sharing their perspective. This reality is similar to the Observer; the difference being that the Empath purely focuses on observing by feeling energy and emotion. Both Superpowers must feel valued, confident and safe to reveal their insightful observations.

For this Superpower, I interviewed Donna Luder, a self-employed body-mind-movement coach. Her work was fundamental in helping me heal a back problem that resurfaces in times of extreme stress. During an extremely painful moment in a session, I noticed her welling up with tears. I knew she was an Empath. As I sensed she was feeling my pain in *her* body.

15 years ago, Donna became aware of her ability. Privately practicing as a body-mind movement coach, she uses Pilates, yoga, and the Franklin Method (™), a mindful body system of alignment and posture. She admits she knew of her empathic abilities as a teenager, but found it a hindrance. When she didn't recognize it as a positive Superpower, she found that empathy could bombard with her emotions and throw her off track. Empaths can find themselves drained if they do not filter incoming information.

How does she access it now? She mirrors what she senses in her clients' bodies. Her empathy informs her how her body would experience that person's sensation. The mirrored feeling appears whenever a client walks into her movement studio and she can feel their sadness, discomfort, or pain. She does not deliberately become empathetic; these feelings are involuntary. At home, she can sense what her family needs from her.

She can even perceive the "dose" of her energy they need. Donna will adjust her doses of support, love or offer space accordingly.

What is crucial for her Superpower? She imagines shutting down emotional sensors in her heart and belly. Using this kind of visualized "filter" is helpful for working with clients as well as in large classes. Larger classes (beyond 12 people) demand too much energy and require a greater level of filtering. When she teaches a yoga class of 30, she sticks to delivering concepts on her agenda that make for a great class experience. To feel everyone's feelings and address each emotional need could potentially overwhelm her with emotion and derail her agenda.

What is her strategy to hone her Superpower? With clients, she chooses to engage mentally with their physical injury to give her information to formulate a treatment plan. She then creates a series of exercises and visualizations to facilitate their pain release and build strength, balance and positive mental imagery for healing. When I worked with her it felt as though she would open a "release valve" for my suffering and pain. I found her guided positive imagery for my back injury helped me reformulate a healthy thought form to replace the fear and pain of my past. Also part of Donna's strategy is to verbalize the desired healthy outcome for her clients and keep them in alignment with that intention.

How does she recharge herself? A lifelong dancer, Donna keeps sticks to a joyful fitness routine that includes dance and yoga. She gets regular bodywork and maintains a healthy diet. To keep herself inspired with her Superpower, Donna surrounds herself with supportive friends and exchanges insights with fellow work colleagues. Her love of learning also renews her Superpower. She goes to Stanford to study cadavers for a deeper insight into human anatomy. Reading books by Joseph Campbell and Carl Jung offer her spiritual perspective.

What is a pitfall of being an Empath? She cannot use this Superpower in a group beyond 12 students as it becomes a liability that draws her into multiple emotions. Empathy is an Achilles Heel because she is drawn to connect with more people but cannot do so without getting engulfed in their emotions.

What blocks Donna's empathy? When someone responds to her insights with hostility she will resort to humor to find common ground. If the person still opposes her, Donna may seek an alternative path to connecting and if they still resist her positivity she will disengage entirely.

Famous Empaths: Bishop Desmond Tutu, Mother Theresa, Thich Nhat Han

Your Affirmation: I listen to others with compassionate understanding.

Conscious Journaling

Take a moment to reflect on your interpretation of the Empath Superpower. Observe what people may have come to your mind as you read this passage. Journal from the prompts of the following questions. Listen to your first response to each and write it down so you can see it. Share the results with someone who is a good listener or someone who could benefit from knowing you better.

1. What qualities or actions do I have that resonate with the Empath Superpower?

2. Who do I know is an Empath and why?

3. What are some ways I could benefit from having an Empath mentor me?

Chapter Summary

Empathy leads to altruism and compassion. It is a Superpower that is vital to understanding others and promoting understanding in relationships and community. When we tap into the feelings of others, we gain valuable information about what can facilitate peaceful journeys and outcomes. Empaths make great healers, health professionals, therapists, and community leaders.

Chapter 11

THE LIMITLESS ACHIEVER: CELEBRATE GOALS

> "Limitations live only in our minds. But if we tune into our imagination, our possibilities become endless."
>
> —Jamie Paolinetti

Limitless Achievers are goal setters and achievers. People with this Superpower move beyond commonly perceived physical, mental and emotional boundaries to achieve their goals. Their ambition leads their vision. Setting new goals excites them.

A Limitless Achiever is capable of sharp focus without distraction. Limitless Achievers know that regular commitment to training fuels each step of their progress toward the goal. Measurable results delight them. Passion is fundamental. Their goal must fulfill a deeper purpose.

They are fearless in nature. Limitless Achievers take calculated risks in moving forward toward their goals. For example, an Olympic athlete will push their body to its capacity *and* meet that same of intensity with adequate recovery time and nourishing diet.

Limitless achievers are motivated by excitement and curiosity to encounter new experiences. This is balanced with their understanding that it takes measured steps to reach their goal. This Superpower is imbued with patience. They value commitment. These attributes propel their progress toward their goals.

THE LIMITLESS ACHIEVER: CELEBRATE GOALS • 65

This Superpower loves to be in the spotlight to inspire others to achieve their best. They model what they believe all people can achieve. They are great coaches and mentors as they enjoy teaching the legacy of goal achievement to others.

My featured Limitless Achiever is Saba Moor-Doucette, a creative woman who shatters limitations. She is an anti-aging and fitness expert, author of five books, creator of two fitness DVDs, and for the past three years, she has been undefeated as a sports-bikini-fitness model in the World Championships. And oh, by the way, she is 74 years old. She has lived life on her terms without heeding constraints.

Since she was quite young, she always went "where [she] knew she was not supposed to go." She never let others' beliefs about women's limitations stop her from doing what she wanted: she was a stunt girl at age 16, rode horses bareback, and was an acrobat in a circus. Saba always thought that if she wanted to do something, she just had to make a plan to get there. During the Vietnam War, she decided to entertain the troops even when people told her it was too dangerous. Throughout her life, Saba has always been on stage in some format, as an actress, comedienne, director, and screenwriter. She always feels completely fearless on stage.

How does she access her Superpower now? Saba feels most energized to use it to address others' needs. She teaches people how to adopt powerful mindsets to achieve their desires. Once, Saba invented an in-car fitness routine called "auto-size" to help a friend who no longer had time to exercise due to his long commute. Hearing about others' blocks encourages her to generate breakthrough solutions. When she is out and about, people often recognize her and say, "You really helped me with your advice." This supercharges her to continue inventing ways to help others.

What is crucial to her Superpower? Saba receives her thoughts straight from the Source, (God, The Divine Source, the Quantum field of infinite potential) allowing such creativity to work through her. Maintaining a daily routine of meditation, a balanced diet, ample rest, and challenging fitness training keeps Saba on target. She focuses on positive thinking throughout her day. Her sense of humor keeps her light. Saba enjoys inspiring others through her writing. She has written books, poetry, and screenplays. She is passionate in her desire to be of service to others. She partners with her husband, Jeff Doucette,(Chapter 15) to teach inspirational workshops to help people breakthrough fear, judgement and limitation.

What strategy does she use to sharpen her Superpower? Whether she's training herself or others, she first concentrates on purpose—the "why." Secondly, she follows her intuition to identify the steps needed to achieve the desired outcome. Next, she believes it will happen for her: Saba visualizes herself doing/receiving it. Focusing powerful thoughts on the core desire is paramount. Her last step is to invite it to happen. She allows the desired outcome to come into fruition. After she receives her desired outcome, she offers gratitude to all who made it possible. Her process has been so successful she wrote the book, *Think it, Do it, Be it* and offers workshops teaching this strategy.

How does she recharge her Superpower? Doing her favorite things rejuvenates her: dancing, playing with her grandchildren, traveling, and doing her LA Talk Radio show: Classic Bikini Divas.

Are there any pitfalls to this Superpower? No. There is always another level of evolution to reach for with joy. Once she achieves a level, she taps into her intuition to illuminate her next challenge. She is dedicated to her Superpower and modeling goal achievement.

What blocks her Superpower? In the past five years, she has not felt blocked. There was a time in her life when she suffered debilitating back pain where she could not get out of bed. Someone suggested, *Healing Back Pain: The Mind-Body Connection* by Dr. John Sarno. Once she discovered her pain originated from an unconscious fear, she reformulated her thoughts and her back pain vanished.

Famous Limitless Achievers: Jackie Chan, Michael Jackson, Gertrude Ederle

***

Your Affirmation: I achieve my goals through committed thought and actions.

Conscious Journaling

Take a moment to reflect on your interpretation of the Limitless Achiever Superpower. Observe what people may have come to your mind as you read this passage. Journal from the prompts of the following questions. Listen to your first response to each and write it down so you can see it. Share the results with someone who is a good listener or someone who could benefit from knowing you better.

1. What qualities or actions do I have that resonate with the Limitless Achiever Superpower?

2. Who do I know is a Limitless Achiever and why?

3. What are some ways I could benefit from having a Limitless Achiever mentor me?

Chapter Summary

Limitless achievers engage life with enthusiasm through goal setting and achievement. They celebrate their progress toward achievement on the way to their goals. They teach us about the joy in surpassing limitation. Their focused commitment to goals teach us the value of diligence and resilience. Limitless achievers make great professional athletes, dancers, academics, engineers, and guides.

Chapter 12

THE OPTIMIST: CELEBRATE POSITIVITY

"Optimism is a happiness magnet. If you stay positive, good things and good people will be drawn to you."

—Mary Lou Retton

This Superpower engages people with encouragement, positivity, and joy. Optimists celebrate accomplishment in all ways. They know how to keep others buoyant even in the throes of disappointment. Optimists view "falling" as part of learning how to walk. They uplift everyone's spirits with their intrinsic glow of gratitude. Optimists grow confident and wise with logged experiences. Optimists can implement strategies to keep people on track and offer sincere praise for accomplishing small tasks along the way. They excel at communication and have a good memory for successes.

Innate Optimists are often created and inspired by Optimists. For example, if parents and grandparents are optimistic about life's challenges as well as life's blessings, it's likely their children will approach life with that Superpower.

Optimists can be captivating and alluring. They model what they feel inside. This Superpower combines their core virtue of honesty with their affirming mindset. Others can feel the that their positive enthusiasm is sincere. I often see Optimists can gather a following with little effort. Their positivity for life magnetizes people to them because they too want to feel good.

People often want to be reminded by an Optimist that there is an upside to a challenging situation. Optimists are undaunted by fear. Their favorable outlook frames every experience. They are motivated by a desire to learn and this beginner mindset opens them up to vast opportunities to improve their knowledge and experience. They embrace life experiences as opportunities to learn more and improve their assets. They simply do not allow negativity to enter their thought sphere. They remain steadfast to the "glass half full." Optimists are great mentors, leaders, teachers and pioneers of new thought movements.

I discovered an Optimist Superpower in a water aerobics class led by a bubbly, enthusiastic instructor, Linda. The first day I began swimming laps at a local pool, I heard (who I thought were) teenagers hooting and hollering in the pool. Imagine my surprise when I walked into the pool and saw all these boisterous shouts coming from retired adults, mostly over the age of 65. Their teacher's encouraging words fueled their ageless passion. Over many months I observed the classes' electric energy and listened to them in the locker room. I realized she inspired them to be positive with each other. Her cheerful encouragement spread to her students. They genuinely care about one another staying uplifted with a bright outlook no matter what challenge they may be facing.

Linda's optimistic outlook started young. Her parents modeled optimism for her. As a child, she was encouraged to do anything she put her mind to. Her parents both modeled this mindset of positivity in their community service and careers. They both were good humored and upheld their children to see the bright side of life. She soon uncovered her optimism through helping others in her 20s and realized how joyful she felt uplifting others in volunteer work.

How does she access her Superpower now? Being of service to others. This includes all her different roles: being a grandma, a water aerobics instructor, and a community service volunteer. All these roles endow her core virtue of gratitude for her blessings. Reinventing her teaching methods by attending fitness symposiums also invigorates her Superpower for her students. The cheering of her class fires up her exuberance.

What is crucial for her Superpower? Her daily commitment to watching the sunrise. Beauty compels her. She loves to exercise daily. She gleans inspiration from self-help books and motivational podcasts. She has bountiful gratitude for all of her daily blessings. Follow-through is also a fundamental ingredient that is specific to Linda's expression of her Superpower. When she makes a promise, she keeps it. She values honesty.

THE OPTIMIST: CELEBRATE POSITIVITY • 71

What is her strategy to hone her Superpower? Fulfilling the needs of others motivates her. When Linda observed a friend's struggle accessing items from her purse that kept falling off her wheelchair, she found a group of quilters to design lovely Velcro bags for those who are wheelchair bound. Volunteering at the Lions Club and Grange Hall also amplify her enthusiasm for life. When she helps those in need, her optimism is nourished.

How does Linda recharge her Superpower? She requires daily exercise, healthy food, and plenty of sleep. Learning yoga in recent years has taught Linda to quiet her mind and learn how to breathe. Her love of learning through books, listening to "driveway stories" on NPR, and watching documentaries rejuvenates her mind.

What is a pitfall of her Superpower? Because she is known as an Optimist, she can feel pressure to appear cheerful even if it does not match her internal feelings. That expectation can fall heavy on her shoulders if she does not truly feel cheerful in the moment.

What blocks her Superpower? Receiving bitter responses to her happy demeanor like, "Why are *you* so happy?" Heavy sadness and pessimism repel her. When she realized her siblings were destructive to her joyful attitude, she gave herself permission to let go of those draining relationships.

Famous Optimists: Louise Hay, Barack Obama, Tom Hanks

***

Your Affirmation: I approach each thought and task with positivity and joy.

Conscious Journaling

Take a moment to reflect on your interpretation of the Optimist Superpower. Observe what people may have come to your mind as you read this passage. Journal from the prompts of the following questions. Listen to your first response to each and write it down so you can see it. Share the results with someone who is a good listener or someone who could benefit from knowing you better.

1. What qualities or actions do I have that resonate with the Optimist?

2. Who do I know is an Optimist and why?

3. What are some ways I could benefit from having an Optimist mentor me?

Chapter Summary

When we tune into the Optimist's channel, anything is possible. When we release negativity and fear, we can tap into unharnessed power to accomplish virtually anything. Gratitude, positivity and eagerness to learn helps us access optimism in our approach each life experience.

Chapter 13

THE INTUITIVE: CELEBRATE INTERNAL GUIDANCE

✦ ✦ ✦

"Intuition helps us understand the light of our soul."

—Heidi Diouf

The Intuitive can perceive events and knowledge below the surface. Intuitives are sensitive to energy, thoughts, emotions and environments. They may lean toward precognition or a extrasensory knowing of a future situation.

In general people can be intuitive in their approach to situations. They may define it as an instinctual feeling or knowing that guided their actions. They may not define it as intuition, rather that their actions were spontaneous, not calculated.

Everyone has the capacity to be the Intuitive. It is a Superpower that can be honed and strengthened with conscious practice. I am aware this is my Superpower and I devoted my life practice and career to my Superpower. Once I became conscious of being an Intuitive, I began using it all the time. My Superpower gained momentum as I stepped out of my comfort zone and began speaking up for my intuition and following my intuition's guidance. As I incorporated using my Intuitive Superpower in my private practice first as an Acupressurist then as an Intuitive Wellness Coach, I became more confident in teaching others to follow their guidance. Eventually, I started a school for intuition: The Spiritual Detective Academy. I wanted to help people use their intuition practically for decision making, for self healing and for understanding the energy that they experience daily.

To develop intuition, I observed that we need to quiet other parts of our mind and body. We have a well developed analytical mind that requires life to have definition and certainty. Our "analyzer" desires things to be "black and white," clear and known. Many aspects of life are not always presented with such precision. The analytical mind can be myopic with its need for facts based on evidence. Intuition taps into knowledge that cannot always be explained. It taps into a greater energetic consciousness/world. I think this is where self doubt can impede our ability to listen to our intuition. I cannot explain how my intuition gathers the information. I *can* explain how I *access* my intuition. My process has been developed over the last 25 years and has become habitual.

Sometimes we have to quiet our emotions as well. They can impede us from the clarity of our intuition. Fear is the most common emotion that divides our analytical mind from our intuitive mind. Any strong emotion can be a block. When we have a strong emotional attachment to one specific outcome this can derail the intuition's guidance. Think of your intuition as a voice. That voice gets drowned out by the incessant cry of an emotion or repeated chatter of the analyzer.

To access my intuition, I created a step by step process to quiet these aspects of the mind and emotions so I could focus solely on intuition. I begin by observing and slowing down my breath. This relaxes me and allows me to listen to my thoughts with less emotion. Then, I visualize I am grounded and balanced like a tree and/or a tripod. As I get more grounded and calm, I send my thoughts to focus toward the back of my head, as though my energy is resting back in a recliner, so to speak. Then I begin to feel a sense of expansiveness and serenity. From this state, I start sensing my intuition in the form of images or words. I allow all this information to be valid. It is a Superpower I have developed over many years so my trust and confidence has grown.

When was I first aware this was my Superpower? When I was five years old. Although I did not have an explanation for how I would know things, I often thought or dreamed about events before they happened. I felt as though learning certain skills was instinctual.

How do I access it now? I explained my method earlier where I breathe deeply and get grounded. Insights may also appear spontaneously, even when I am not in meditation. When I am alone hiking, practicing yoga, or immersed in water, I will pick up on all kinds of hunches about people, animals, my community, and global events. When I am teaching, intuition provides a sense flow and congruency. I get an instant feeling when a yoga student is out of alignment or when they misunderstand a concept. I sense it through a sudden tension in my body or I will "hear" the name of the student who is out of alignment. I also intuitively coach my clients doing readings by phone or online. Whether the person is local or overseas, I sense imagery about where they are emotionally, mentally, and physically—often before they explain their circumstances. In a session, I tune into how I can use my intuition to access my client's highest and greatest good. Once I set that intention to help them, the information flows through my intuition. I listen and share these insights with them.

What is crucial to my Superpower? I must focus and breathe with the present moment. I receive pivotal information when I tune in to the 'now.' However, because I am in a trancelike state when reading others, I cannot retain the information and must immediately share and record it. I am also devoted to breathing, meditation, and daily grounding practices. Being well rested, nourished, and hydrated is vital. When I am teaching or doing a reading, lighting/decor must be calm to remain clear of distractions.

What is my strategy to hone my Superpower? My committed meditation practice helps me clarify or filter incoming information. I create a visual, mental strategy to prevent distracting thoughts. I picture energy centers or "chakras" in my body being filled with an intended energy, filtered from discordant energy, and protected from negativity. My "filter" represents my intention to allow desired energy in and keep out distracting and undesirable energy/emotion.

How do I recharge? Regular practice of Hatha yoga, hiking, swimming, dancing, listening to music, reading and journaling nourish me. Music inspires me. Seeing water and watching birds invigorates my creativity. The sounds of owls are especially transcendent for me.

What amplifies my Superpower? Being in or around water amplifies my intuition. In addition, I created a community at my studio where intuition is welcomed and encouraged. When I am with my community, my intuition resonates with a louder volume. I observe this happens for my students and clients as well.

What are the pitfalls of being intuitive? I sense the negative and limiting connotation of being called a "psychic" so I avoid using this label for my intuitive work. Most people think psychics predict the future. I "read" what is right in front of me, right now. I believe we can always choose to reshape our future. Another pitfall is when people override listening to their own intuition for mine. I prefer they listen to their intuitive guidance to serve them. An additional pitfall of being an Intuitive is picking up on too much information. If I forget to filter, protect, or clear myself of incoming information, I feel exhausted. Often when I get a lot of incoming information spontaneously I may feel overwhelmed. Sometimes I feel an obligation to share an intuitive insight with someone but feel awkward because my hunch was spontaneous and sometimes out of context.

What blocks my Superpower? Being on a plane can sometimes dull my intuitive insights. Dehydration and sleep deprivation can block my clarity. Self-doubt is my biggest block. If I allow my fear of judgment or my desire to be flawless to prevail, it keeps me from speaking up about my insights. Negative mindsets around intuition can sometimes prevent me from sharing my insights. As I have aged with my Superpower, I rarely let someone's limitation prevent my intuition from being a lamp for others.

Famous Intuitives: Caroline Myss, Meryl Streep, Martha Graham

***

Your Affirmation: I celebrate and share my powerful, intuitive insights.

Conscious Journaling

Take a moment to reflect on your interpretation of the Intuitive Superpower. Observe what people may have come to your mind as you read this passage. Journal from the prompts of the following questions. Listen to your first response to each and write it down so you can see it. Share the results with someone who is a good listener or someone who could benefit from knowing you better.

1. What qualities or actions do I have that resonate with the Intuitive Superpower?

2. Who do I know is an Intuitive and why?

3. What are some ways I could benefit from having an Intuitive mentor me?

Chapter Summary

Intuition is a Superpower that grants us access our inner wisdom and guidance. It offers expansive awareness concerning many aspects of our life's circumstances. Our intuition helps us discern what resonates with us and keeps us in alignment with our desired intentions for a conscious journey. Intuitives make great health practitioners, healers, visionaries, writers, and health professionals.

Chapter 14

MANAGING FEAR

"Don't let fear paralyze you. Let it motivate you."

—Unknown

If you knew you had a Superpower, why would you try to block it? We encounter many critical moments in our life, and sometimes we must make choices that will powerfully impact an end result. Uncertainty of outcome can trigger fears. These are "dig-deep" moments when our Superpowers reveal themselves. There's a brilliant example of this pivotal moment in the movie, *Wonder Woman*. She had a choice to use her Superpowers to make or break the course of a battle. In this scene, she witnesses intense bloodshed from a destructive attack on her village. Missiles and ammunition bombard her small team of soldiers and she feels the surrounding anguish and fear—her Superpower as an Empath soon overwhelms her. Her decision to use her otherworldly Superpowers (blocking bullets, speed, etc.) is compelled by her passion to end suffering. Despite being outnumbered, she steps into the line of fire as an Activator to inspire her allies to defeat the enemy. This motivates her soldiers to become Limitless Achievers, charging toward victory.

Superpowers weave into the fabric of our identity and purpose. Sometimes we can overlook them and take our Superpower for granted. You may rely on your Superpower only in response to a deadline. You may only use your Superpower in crisis. You may know it exists, but not use it unless absolutely necessary. I often see a pattern in myself and others: we are the masters of getting in our way. Getting through your blocks means getting through your ego, which may be rooted in fear of success or failure.

I have observed these top 10 limiting beliefs that can block our Superpowers:

1) You think you are not enough.
2) You believe feeling powerful is out of your comfort zone.
3) You think you will be judged for being masterful in your Superpower.
4) You believe you will recreate a negative outcome from your past.
5) You think you are not skillful to handle the consequences of your actions.
6) You believe you will not measure up to the expectations of others.
7) You fear the future is negative.
8) You fear success.
9) You fear failure.
10) You think you are too comfortable, too old, too (fill in the blank) to change.

These sabotaging beliefs can lead to these sabotaging behaviors:

1) Procrastination.
2) Over-giving without healthy boundaries.
3) Aversion to taking action on blocks.
4) Plateauing in your Superpower by staying in your comfort zone.
5) Overwork without regard to physical needs.
6) Creating distractions that pull you away from decisive action.
7) Not growing in a job, relationship, business, or situation and becoming creatively stagnant.

We create these sabotaging thoughts and behaviors to navigate around fear rather than accepting it and moving through it. The reasoning behind fear is usually not in the present moment. Fearful thoughts usually relate to the past or future unless there really is a speeding bus about to hit you. Most fears are born from not being where we are all most powerful: in the present moment.

Many years ago, I was doing a massage in a beautiful conference center on the California coast. My client forgot to tell me she had a port around her collarbone (used for delivering chemotherapy), so I was surprised when I saw it. I was stunned she could forget to tell me something so significant. She explained to me she was diagnosed with Stage 4 breast cancer and was set to receive chemotherapy via the port. Her approach to her fear of cancer was to change her thoughts about the disease. She saw cancer as living cells in her body that did not belong there. By telling the cells that "they were not bad, they just did not belong in this body," she sent them away and continued to do so until her next doctor's appointment. In her following CT scan, the doctors found no trace of cancer anywhere. There was no need to receive chemo, but she didn't have time to remove the port before we met at the conference. This example profoundly changed my ideas about addressing common fears, especially ones carrying a strong emotional charge in our society. Cancer is probably on the list of top 5 fears for most people. Imagine how powerful we are with our thoughts and how we can heal imbalances in our lives when we think with fearless positivity.

Have you ever heard of these fear acronyms? F.E.A.R. as in Forget Everything And Run or False Evidence Appearing Real. What fuels fear? Uncertainty, past, and future thoughts. When I first accepted myself as an Intuitive, I feared if I listen to my intuition, I could be wrong. My future thoughts were charged with this fear: what if my insight negatively influences an outcome? My past fears looked for evidence of judgment. I used to call a friend, Elise, when I felt stuck between two mindsets: fear-based self-invalidation or trust-based intuition. Her candid humor would break the spell of my overthinking. She would answer the phone saying, "This is 1-800-dial-a-validation, I am your operator, Elise. How may I validate you?" My compassionate "operator" would call out the F.E.A.R. and remind me of the truth. With compassionate neutrality, she would identify the origin of the fear, and offer support to navigate my mindset back into present reality. With supportive validation and affirmations I was able to shift my first False Evidence Appearing Real to Face Everything And Rise.

Realize that the friends, allies, and colleagues you surround yourself with can support the expression of your Superpower. Support and accountability keep you in line with the truth and "the now" for better results. Catching and shifting your negative, self-deprecating thoughts to the positive must become a habit. Sometimes I feared asking for help in writing this book because I thought I would inconvenience others. When others ask *me* for help, however, I feel good supporting them. I have to remind myself that by asking someone to help me, I am giving them the opportunity to feel generous and altruistic.

Superpower Fear Busting Tip

TRANSFORM	F.orget	TO	F.ace
	E.verything		E.verything
	A.nd		A.nd
	R.un		R.ise

WITH AFFIRMATIONS:

I embrace every challenge with optimism.
I have all the courage and knowledge I need to take action beyond my fear.

Belonging to a focus group in business, spirituality, or physical fitness is another way to conquer fear by recognizing, activating, and using your Superpower. Sharing your Superpower with a group can keep you on target and motivate fellow members to do the same. The group keeps its community fear-free and "Superpower-accountable."

Gaining Traction

"Traction" is defined on dictionary.com as "the extent to which a product, idea, etc., gains popularity or acceptance." It is synonymous with the word "grip." Once we master a Superpower, we can create traction. We get a grip on our fear by repeating the steps that integrate the new Superpower actions. Practicing motor skills over and over again garners finesse in movement. Practice leads to certainty and initiates momentum.

When learning a new skill set, we often do not master it on our first go. We open a neural pathway the first time we understand a concept, e.g., the first time we learn to parallel park a car. Every time after that, we can finesse a different aspect, making it smoother. Our thoughts and movement increase acceptance to new information and skill sets. Practice fuels progress.

Apply that same concept to mastering fear. The first step you take out of your comfort zone opens that pathway. Each step after that creates traction—your mind starts to accept and become familiar with the new territory. The more traction we gain, the more our confidence grows. The first time you try meditation, your thoughts may wander or your body may wriggle like a fish. Each time afterward becomes easier because your mind and body get comfortable with the experience. Recall Saba, our Limitless Achiever in Chapter 2. When she participated in her first bikini modeling championship, she didn't know what to expect. After she lost her first competition, she realized what she could improve in her training and performances. She applied the new knowledge and began winning titles.

Every time you step out of your comfort zone you need to acknowledge your uncertainty. Focus on positivity so you can adhere to the new pathway. A successful path starts with your breath and your thoughts. Recall what it feels like to be excited. Then tune into what it feels like to be scared. These are similar feelings in your body. The first—excitement—stimulates breath, the second—fear—withholds breath. To dissipate fear, start with slow, deep, and steady breaths. Tune into the inhale and exhale equally. This action will slow your thoughts and relax your body. Once in a state of calm, we can tap into an ease of expansion and creativity.

Superpower tip

Fear is Excitement WITHOUT the breath.
To dissipate fear: take full, deep breaths.

Tune into your thoughts. Be aware when your thoughts restrict possibilities. Notice when you wander towards painful memories. Try to re-sort your thoughts with compassion as you practice stepping out of a 'thought comfort zone.' Allow more volume to positive thoughts than negative ones. Play with opening your thoughts to boundless opportunity. I like to do this by saying to myself, "What would it be like to experience _____?" Fill in the blank with experiences you desire but have been too afraid to ask for or receive.

> **Gaining Traction on Fear**
>
> Take one step out of comfort zone.
> Acknowledge uncertainty.
> Be grateful for your Superpower.
> Switch fear to excitement with relaxed breathing.
> Swap self defeating thoughts for motivational ones.

Ask and Receive Your Breakthrough

Cultivating a breakthrough of fear requires honest vulnerability—an admission we are stuck in our fear. We must recognize our limiting patterns of being and doing are no longer working for our endeavors. Just because we identify our Superpowers does not mean they always exist. You must continue to feed your Superpower with new tools, inspiration, and education. These nutrients will keep your Superpowers nourished, preventing plateaus and a depletion of enthusiasm. Lack of growth in your Superpower is also a type of block. We can get too comfortable with the routine use of a Superpower and become bored, apathetic or take it for granted.

Once you realize you are stuck in a pattern of fearful thinking, start by asking with curiosity "Why?" Write down the first thing that comes to your mind. Feel the feelings that come with that realization. Go straight into those feelings rather than resisting or avoiding them. Breathe deep, full breaths. Let your fear be as big and "bad" as it can be in your mind, heart or body as you breathe into it. Stay with it. Several things can happen when we do this:

1) We can see that it is only a thought that compels this emotion and the thought can be changed.

2) We can become aware of our choice to feel fear *and* that we can make a different choice.

3) We can be conscious that once we breathe into it, that fear starts to dissolve and eventually go away.

4) We can grasp the idea that fear can be a moment that we are "nursing." We have our breath and our choice to release the moment and harness our Superpower move through it.

5) We can recall the friends and colleagues that can support our breaking through this fear barrier.

6) We can tap into our creativity to expand us beyond the deadlock of fear.

Imagine several instances of what overcoming this moment of fear would look or feel like. Ask yourself "What would it be like to feel confident and courageous?" Allow yourself to dream about it. Then acutely listen to everything around you to receive the answer. Start paying closer attention to what people say when you are out in the world. Notice what you hear on the radio. Read inspirational authors, keeping your breakthrough needs on the forefront. It may be helpful to brainstorm with a respected mentor or friend with the Superpower you need to move through this fear.

Superpower tip to Breakthrough Fear

Acknowledge the fear.
Ask yourself why are you afraid?
Breathe slow, deep and steady breaths into your fear.
Ask for a breakthrough.
Seek friend to support you.
Seek knowledge and inspiration to move you.

I once learned from a first nation shaman that if you want to transform something in your life, you have to start walking different paths. After learning some transformative healing concepts, he encouraged us to drive home a different way, one we have never gone before. He asked us to become hyper-aware of what signs and scenery we saw on the way home. I did this many times as I was writing this book. I would hear something I needed to hear on the radio. I would see something inspirational by hiking a different trail, and it would spark a new idea for the book. I would hear something in a conversation that was an answer to a question I had. It was incredible how they all resonated with what I needed to know. My epiphany was knowing I needed to ask and then to listen, on all frequencies, to receive my answers.

After you have identified the source of your fear, use this strategy to foster a Superpower Fear Breakthrough:

1) Go to the library or do an online search, seeking new authors that resonate with your desired Superpower.

2) Check out meetup groups, telesummits, webinars, and podcasts that relate to the Superpower you are growing.

3) Watch an inspiring documentary that demonstrates your desired Superpower in action.

4) Listen with expanded awareness for guidance to your Superpower purpose.

5) Be open to the delivery of answers. They may appear unconventionally and unexpectedly (i.e., through a song on a radio station, podcast, nature, or in an overheard conversation).

6) Write about yourself in present time as if you have already integrated your new Superpower. Write your Superpower story with details you are willing to experience. Sharing this story with a close friend allows you to hear your positive affirmation.

7) Once you receive an insight or epiphany, change the way you go home, to school or work, and pay attention to your observations on this new path.

Each step boosts your confidence and invites momentum toward breakthroughs. Practice and repetition will meld these new thoughts and actions into your consciousness. Keep tuning into your environment and be open to all the ways (symbolic or actual) your breakthrough may come to you. Be willing to receive and wait patiently for an answer that resonates with you.

Words Matter

Our throat is a powerful place. Through words, we express our truth and speak up for what we believe. If you say something repeatedly, you begin to believe it, and your actions will reflect those words. For example, if you say, "I always fall off my mountain bike when I ride this trail," you will likely fall off your bike on that trail every time. If you change your thoughts and your words toward staying on your bike, you will start finding ways to remain on your bike throughout your ride.

Speaking to your fear is a powerful method to master fear. Speaking your fears out loud can allow you to decide how much you want to continue to invest time and energy into them. When you are with a group and you speak your fears out loud, everyone gets the opportunity to release that fear too. It takes constant word monitoring to manage a deeply rooted fear. I say things out loud like, "Cancel that thought" or "Delete that thought and rewrite" when I hear myself thinking or saying a fear-based limitation. Change any habitual, limiting thoughts that begin with "I never can do ___ or I always fear doing ___." Instead say, "Up until now I haven't mastered this fear, yet I am willing to establish a new mindset to overcome it." The way we use words to express ourselves also shows us what we believe. I invite you to consciously choose the thoughts and words that truly express your greatness, your light, your Superpowers.

Conscious Journaling

Read and reflect on the following questions; remain open to your first answer to each question. Write it down so you can see it, then share the results with someone who is a good listener or someone who could benefit from knowing you.

1. How has fear limited my growth?

2. Do I let fear stand between me and my greatest desires?

3. How has fear served me in the past?

4. How does fear serve me now?

5. Notice *where* you feel the fear in your body regarding a situation that you desire a different feeling. "Talk" to that place in your body where you feel the fear and ask the fear why it's there?

6. Now that you have clarity on the "why" of your fear, write down some places and people you can seek for your inspirational breakthrough. Trust your intuition about the Superpower that can help you move through this moment of fear.

Chapter Summary

We are all familiar with the feeling of fear. When we acknowledge and face fearful thoughts, we build mastery for the next time we encounter fear. It is important to challenge fearful mindsets and beliefs because they are rarely based on the present moment and they hold us hostage from transformation. Tuning into the breath shifts fear to excitement and aligns us with the power of now. This shift opens us up to virtues like courage, enthusiasm and curiosity. As we acquire new Superpowers or take ownership of our dominant one, we allow courage and decisive action to overcome any fear that could inhibit our full potential.

CHAPTER 15

HOW TO APPROACH FAILURE

"The greatest glory in living lies not in never falling, but in rising every time we fall."

—Nelson Mandela

If we think we are failing, we may feel like we are merely reacting to a series of collisions, rather than choosing our experiences. In these moments, we may think of our current self or situation as a failed cause. We often misinterpret failure; however, it can encourage us to positively reconstruct our lives. For me, misperceived failures became mile markers, indicating I am on the verge of a breakthrough. Capsized circumstances ultimately gave birth to new ideas which result in more successful outcomes.

After I wrote this book, I encountered challenges and what felt like blocks to my progress in publishing. Edits, revisions, glitches in technology, missed emails with directions...I needed to redefine failure. I came up with this acronym: F.irst A.ttempt I.n L.earning U.nexpected R.ich E.xperiences. I see F.irst A.ttempt I.n L.earning as: adopt a beginner mindset, be open to the lesson. The U.nexpected R.ich E.xperience is where I forgive myself for being attached to a certain outcome. I shift that mindset to being *grateful for the richness of what is.*

Reframe F.A.I.L.U.R.E			
See it as:	F.irst A.ttempt I.n L.earning U.nexpected R.ich E.xperiences	**By Infusing:**	Openness to Learning Forgiveness Gratitude

For over 20 years, I witnessed this phenomenon as a doula (birth coach) for women who desired a drug-free birth. We collaborated on the birth plan beforehand, then followed pre-planned steps throughout labor (strategies for birthing positions, meditation, and breathing techniques) to address pain.

The most painful part of labor, the transition phase, is also the shortest. Contractions are more intense but last for less time. When the laboring mom reaches the threshold of pain and fatigue, she is often near the end of this challenging time, right before the pushing phase. Even though they were forewarned, some of my clients wanted to toss out the "drug-free birth plan" when they get to this phase. *They want the pain meds.* The intensity of the pain amplifies their fearful emotional state, which also increases their fear of failing the natural birth plan.

To address this fear, I created a strategy to change the atmosphere. I dimmed the lights, applied aromatherapy oils, and changed a laboring position in order to change the woman's perception of the pain. I would then lean in at eye level, synchronizing our breathing, and squeezing her partner's hand. Together we affirmed her of her strength, reassuring her that she is almost done. Within moments, the baby would be born.

This birth metaphor can offer hope when we reach a threshold of fatigue and pain in our lives. We may tell ourselves we are failing and that we should give up. This is the time we most urgently need support: a trusted mentor or friend could help us get through the last push. They can also change the environment of thoughts and feelings to alter the perspective from failure to triumph. This can "birth" us to the next stage of evolution.

Be aware of your self-defeating thoughts; this can prevent you from an overwhelming fear of failure. Breathing fuller breaths with awareness synchronizes your thoughts with the truth of the present moment. We may overlook the importance of conscious thought, but it creates the possibility to change. If we can act on our self-defeating thoughts—choosing not to rationalize them, then we may take the first steps toward positive, decisive action.

To shed light on our inner critic, I interviewed my friend, Jeff Doucette. For the past 30 years, Jeff has been working in Hollywood as a television and movie actor. He also works as a spiritual counselor at The Center for Spiritual Living, where he serves as an advocate to help others overcome lifestyle, career and relationship blocks. Jeff attributes his acting and coaching success to his combined Superpowers of Observer and Innovator.

Jeff says thoughts of failure are like seeing a pixelated picture: it doesn't resonate with what you desire to see clearly. During dry patches in his acting career, he found himself engulfed with negativity. To protect himself, he started blaming everyone else. His thought was, "If I am not succeeding, it must be someone else's fault." But, when this didn't get him anywhere, he decided to make a change in himself. He would find funny ways to gain attention. He would convert his frustration of unemployment into witty, sarcastic parodies. He still felt disappointed internally, but he started entertaining people with his comedic routine. Even though laughter fed his ego, he still wanted people to recognize his value as an actor. Consequently, he started consciously reaffirming his talent and value as an actor. Once he continually reaffirmed to himself and others that work was going to come, he received more calls for auditions and work streamed in.

He also shared another insight about his approach to failure. It relates to what he calls his "inner critic." When creativity is not flowing, Jeff sees that he is out of balance with his current reality of the moment. His inner critic wants to be right, in control, and run the show. Jeff defines the inner critic as the negative voice in his head that sees life as limited. When this inner critic senses failure, it starts reminding him what he did wrong and says, "You should have done this, Jeff." The inner critic's words veil what is valuable in the present moment, so he must redirect his attention towards his thoughts, attitudes, and beliefs about the current situation. From there, he takes ownership of his beliefs to match the reality he wants to experience.

As I began to use Jeff's strategy, I became more aware of my inner critic. It started coming up in all of these ugly ways—even when I was writing this chapter! My inner critic thought perfection was a precedent to writing a book. It said things like, "Who do you think you are? *Becoming a writer at this age?*" One negative thought led to another, and they became so powerful I stopped writing for a couple of weeks. I felt swallowed by self-doubt. It seemed to eat up all of my encouraging words. So, I began Jeff's strategy: observing my thoughts but not becoming them. I thanked my inner critic for its input, then firmly chose a more affirmative thought (we will explore more of this process in Chapter 19: Thought Swap). I realized that I needed to thank my inner critic's negativity because it awakened my desire for change.

Looking at it from the big picture, an inner critic can result in a better version of ourselves. Initiating change with gratitude expands our vision beyond the "I should've done this, I should've done that." (I now call this "bull-shoulda.") Calling out the inner critic with a sense of humor can also help you soften and forgive yourself.

> **Superpower Tip to Curb your Inner Critic**
> Use humor and laughter to break tension and negativity.

Here's a breakdown of the steps to overcome your inner critic:

1) Realize you are out of balance and unhappy with your current reality.

2) Observe the thoughts of your inner critic.

3) Own that you created and believed those thoughts.

4) Thank your inner critic for making it obvious you are unhappy with your current reality.

5) Use your sense of humor with your inner critic.

6) Forgive your inner critic. Practice the Hawaiian Ho'oponopono forgiveness practice (also found in Chapter 6) by saying, "I am sorry. Please forgive me. I love you. Thank you."

7) Change the inner critic's thoughts to align with your desired reality.

8) Affirm that everything you need to know is in the present moment.

Jeff's strategy converts negative thoughts to affirming thoughts to obtain desired outcomes. In his example, he changes the thought of "why can't I get any acting jobs? There must be something wrong with me!" to "I am recreating the best way to present myself as a working actor," and "work is coming my way." He suggests we must act as if we are already receiving the desired outcome. Imagine what it would feel like in your body, then reboot your thoughts, attitudes, and beliefs to match that aspiration. This "changes the pixels" of your perspective to match what you desire to experience. He calls this "acting as if." In his example, he would set up daily routines as if he was working. Commitment to the new thought is crucial to change old beliefs.

With his Observer Superpower, Jeff sees people often adopting what he calls "the winning attitude." While this attitude has taken him far in life, it has also impeded his growth.

Sometimes those with winning attitudes set themselves up for failure because they are impervious to change. Accustomed to comfort of what "wins," they fear if they change, they will risk losing that familiar outcome. The uncertainty of the unknown can stop them from trying to improve their attitude.

Jeff knew he needed to adopt a different attitude to attract more work. As an Observer, he remained neutral about his situation so he could reshape his thoughts, attitudes, and beliefs. Then, he tapped into his Innovator Superpower to revise his winning attitude. By repeating positive affirmations, and surrounding himself with positive people, he was able to reap the rewards of prosperous flow of paid acting jobs.

Here's how to use Jeff's strategy to transform your perspective of failure:

1) Observe your thoughts. Avoid labeling a thought with a judgment (i.e. negative, lame, limiting, etc.).

2) Own your thought. You created it. You can UN-create it if it does not match how you want to feel. Take ownership of each thought so you have the power to edit your mindset.

3) Give thanks for your awareness. This is your opportunity to create something new that resonates with your path.

4) Change your thought to a different, more expansive one. I like doing this by thinking, "What would it feel like if I felt supported in this situation? What kind of support would I like to receive?"

5) Act "as if" you are already believing the new thought, doing the new action, or receiving what you desire. For instance: "My work as an actor continues to prosper. I feel fulfilled in all ways as an actor."

6) Remain in the present moment with your breath. This offers countless opportunities to come up with new thoughtful possibilities. When you release past and future thoughts, you release limitation. The past already happened. The future is created by seizing the power of the present moment.

Assimilate this strategy by making it a daily habit. Make time each day to clear self-defeating thoughts and deliberately monitor your thoughts.

As we heighten our awareness of our patterns of thinking we realize how possible it is to reframe our thoughts on failure. Once we see that failure as an unexpected result we take the negativity out of it. This lightens the burden and makes the journey of change much more joyful and exhilarating. Loving the learning process with supportive people that can make us laugh, can pull us out of patterns of negative overthinking.

✦ ✦ ✦

Conscious Journaling

Read and reflect on the following questions. Remain open to your first answer to each question. Write it down so you can see it. Share the results with someone who is a good listener or someone who could benefit from knowing you.

1. Observe one negative thought you had today. Write one gratitude for this thought. Write down a positive thought to replace this negative one.

2. Think of a moment in your past you called yourself a "failure." How did you respond to that failure? Write a Superpower you would use now to reframe your response to the "failure"?

3. Recall one of your best moments of goal achievement. Identify one negative thought you erased to get there. Recall how you replaced that negative thought.

4. Notice when you hear your inner critic's voice NOW in your thoughts. How might you reframe a negative thought into a positive one?

5. Tune into a current relationship where you experience conflict.
Observe your inner critic's feedback about this.
Write one gratitude for your inner critic's feedback.
What is one positive thought you could replace the negative one with?

6. Name one way you can "act as if" you already have what you want in this relationship.

$$\begin{array}{|l|}\hline \\ \\ \\ \\ \hline\end{array}$$

7. Focus your thoughts on a current reality where you desire a different experience. Observe your current thoughts and jot down a few.

$$\begin{array}{|l|}\hline \\ \\ \\ \\ \hline\end{array}$$

8. State your gratitude for these thoughts. Create some new thoughts that resonate with how you prefer to feel about this experience.

$$\begin{array}{|l|}\hline \\ \\ \\ \\ \hline\end{array}$$

9. Write a couple of different variations of you already having the new experience.

10. What Superpower can support your "acting as if" you already have a desired experience?

Chapter Summary

Redefine the word FAILURE as a First Attempt In Learning Unexpected Rich Experiences. You may have encountered an unexpected bump on the road and you can accept it with self-love. Receiving support and accountability helps us stay on track toward progress. Regular meditations, conscious breathing, and affirmations effectively eliminates limiting perspectives on failure.

CHAPTER 16

ADDING AND COMBINING SUPERPOWERS

"Yesterday I was clever, so I wanted to change the world. Today I am wise, so I am changing myself."

—Jalal-uddin Rumi

As we open our minds to assimilating more Superpowers, we see ourselves differently. In developing these powers, it is important we create space in our lives to receive compelling insights: think about all the ways this new Superpower may serve us, our relationships, and our projects.

Learning New Superpowers

When we want to learn new Superpowers, we must first acknowledge how they will help us serve our needs. Secondly, it's a good idea to map out a daily routine to ensure you make time to develop these new Superpowers. Any learning process requires patience, so set a deadline for yourself, and at that time, determine if you need to call in somebody who embodies that Superpower to help you. They can propel your transformation by teaching you their habits, traits, and actions. They may give you exercises to reinforce those traits and keep you accountable until your desired Superpower is activated.

Additionally, you could learn a new Superpower in a group setting. For instance, improve your Container power by taking a class in financial planning. Join a fitness community to collaboratively goal-set for optimum health. In a group, you will be surrounded with people also learning that Superpower, thus amplifying your learning, ownership, and purpose. I created a group program to help people develop their Superpowers knowing that their growth and progress would be amplified by each other.

I used to believe I could never get organized in my home office. It was like walking on the "dark side of the moon." I got so desperate I called in a Superpower that completely repelled me—the Container. At the time, I falsely believed Containers only involved limiting rules, rigidity, and what I feared even worse: judgment. Cecile, my Container-friend, proved me wrong and taught me a Container organization system. Her mentoring improved my daily time management, and our weekly appointments kept me accountable. Each time we met, she shared a new, helpful tool. I downed the "Container Kool-Aid" and became a master of my version of the Container. I realized the only thing holding me back was my limiting belief about my ability to become a Container. Once you master a Superpower you once believed was unattainable, it not only builds your confidence but becomes exhilarating!

Negative thinking can derail your acquisition of new Superpowers. Avoid making a Superpower unachievable with a negative attitudes. In my example, my first step was to acknowledge my apprehension of Containers based on a negative perception. Then I forgave myself for those negative thoughts. I found a compassionate version of that Superpower and collaborated with Cecile to attain it. As I committed to the steps she designed specifically for me, I transformed into my version of the Container and added it to my Superpower bank account.

There are many ways to develop a new Superpower. Perhaps you admire someone with a unique Superpower in your social circle. Maybe you are like me: repelled by a certain Superpower because of some limiting thought. Remember, an expert mentor can provide tips and strategies to ease adoption of the Superpower. Be open to establishing your incarnation of that Superpower. In my example, I chose to commit to my specific version of a Container.

During my interview with Jeff from Chapter 4, he explained a process he used to take on new Superpowers spontaneously as an actor. The process is a conscious application of "acting as if method." When shooting a scene, the actors are telling a story. The director determines which behaviors are needed to tell that story. When Jeff hears the directions, he internally gets a feel for what motivates his character. He imagines how his character would behave (confident, passionate, exhausted, etc.), then if the director needs to change something in the scene, Jeff improvises and makes a different choice for the character's actions. He combines the requested motivation with a behavior and acts as if it already is so. He applies this mindset to his life off-camera when he needs to change his behaviors to match his current ambitions. We can also apply Jeff's method to developing new Superpowers.

"Acting as if method" to develop new Superpowers:

1) Choose the Superpower that matches your desired outcome.

2) Decide what motivates that Superpower's action.

3) Imagine yourself as that Superpower.

4) Commit to the Superpower behavior by acting as if you are that Superpower. Phrase your words in present time.

5) Integrate that behavior into your thoughts, beliefs, and actions.

6) Be grateful for the process of flowering in your version of that Superpower.

7) Deposit this gain to your "Superpower bank account."

Combining Two or More Superpowers

We can use several Superpowers simultaneously, depending on the circumstances. When I am teaching meditation and yoga, I am a Container who holds the peaceful environment and keeps my student's poses in proper alignment. At the same time, I am the Synthesizer that balances the peaceful energy of the class with my poses, words, and voice inflection. I also remain the constant Observer of their breath, alignment, and movement to keep them in symmetry.

I follow a thought process when I set my Superpower intention for each creation. As I create, I keep tuning into what is needed and what Superpower might fulfill that need (intentions and tasks). In writing this book, I needed a system to guide me through each step, so first, I sought a Container. I participated in a workshop where I was provided a template and system to guide my creativity. As I got into the heart of writing, I needed experts to represent each Superpower. I became an Observer of everyday people in different environments. I matched their dominant actions with appropriate Superpowers. These observations led me to find representatives with clear examples of the traits and behaviors I needed to illustrate. As I continued writing I needed to become more aware of what my reader might be thinking or feeling. The Empath fit that need. I polled people about their experiences of fear and failure to understand what they were feeling. I then created strategies to overcome prevailing mindsets about fear, failure, etc.

In summary, we can tune into our intention and evaluate what Superpower we need to achieve with each objective. It helps to reflect on the present moment with your breath, so you stay tapped into your power.

I interviewed a woman who uses several Superpowers in her business. After our interview, I concluded her development of new Superpowers contains a similar process to mine. Gia is an acupuncturist, health & wellness coach, bodyworker, and business owner of 22 years. The Superpowers she puts to use daily are the Container, Innovator, Synthesizer, and Observer. She explained the adaptation of her Superpowers and how they have blossomed over time.

Gia loves to learn. This love of learning compels her to acquire new Superpowers when her life requires it. Being a Container comes naturally to her and she styles her home and office to create balance, peace, and flow. The Container best describes her inherent skills of organization and creating healthy regimens for her clients. This is a Superpower that comes easily to her. When she became a bodyworker, she learned a few modalities for massage. She followed their protocols as a Container but found some modalities fell short in helping clients with rare conditions. When her training in one system fell short, she realized she needed to become an Innovator. Gia would research trends and results of different teachings on nutrition, herbs, and treatments until she discovered a teacher who provided that coveted knowledge. Then she studied and got certified in that modality. In time, she became an Innovator of several alternative therapies. She became an expert on when and how to apply specific methods to unique cases for optimal results.

As her Acupuncture practice progressed, she learned to develop her skills as an Observer, to see beneath her patient's symptoms and identify the root cause. Her method of charting a patient's feedback helped her log information, observe changes, and evaluate a treatment plan's effectiveness. Becoming an Observer was a natural progression in her growth as a practitioner. Now she combines all forces, carefully observing her client's lifestyles, symptoms, and the big picture of their ultimate goals.

As she has grown in her personal and professional relationships, she has found it essential to integrate her Superpower of Synthesizer. It is necessary for her to balance her drive to acquire more knowledge and her need for fun and relaxation. Her Synthesizer Superpower developed over the last 15 years as a result of her need for balance. She had to abandon the limiting belief that she needed to be perfect. Self acceptance has led her to be more compassionate with herself. Now she opts for a more self-loving inward gaze which allows her to be in sync with all her Superpowers.

Gia continually seeks knowledge for growth and evolution. Plateauing is not an option. For her to feel expansive in her Superpowers, she practices new meditation and health practices on herself. As she modifies her diet, exercise, or yoga practices, she marks her changes. Gia will not recommend a therapy or herbal medicine unless she has personally tried it. Her process of experimentation hones her Innovator Superpower. The need for balance as a Synthesizer enables her to model wellness to her clients. Her curiosity and love of learning inspire her to seize opportunities to improve her health and education. If she senses she is stagnating with growth she feels compelled to seek new knowledge and inspiration.

What fires up her Superpower combination? To be in service to others. When asked to team up with a friend, family member, or client for transformation, her fire sparks. She feels passionate about masterminding their change with all four Superpowers. Gia taps into all four to reboot a client's health, revamp a friend's marketing plan, or help a friend redecorate a room. She combines three Superpowers when consulting a friend about their product launch into large-scale markets. She observes the demand for his product(Observer), syncs the strengths of each person on their team(Synthesizer) and organizes their ideas for growth (Container). At the time of our interview, Gia relished the idea of partnering with innovative health practitioners to establish a cutting-edge health and wellness center in Marin County, CA. She saw from the Innovator's perspective how this spa could improve self-care practices. She created a platform to join forces with exceptional practitioners to offer clients optimal wellness. By the time of book printing, Gia's Resonance Spa was completed.

How does she maintain balance with all of her Superpowers? To fuel positivity for her Superpowers, Gia uses a mindful meditation practice to balance her mental and emotional states. This maintains her awareness of her thoughts and a positive mindset. She also focuses on maintaining her physical health to hone her Superpowers. Her daily regimen of exercise, yoga, balanced nutrition, herbal supplements and plenty of rest keeps her in alignment. If her routine is off-kilter, she becomes a wilted flower. It is essential for her to make time for herself to laugh and be social so she does not get caught up with stress or overwork.

What challenges does she face with her Superpower combination? One challenge Gia encounters with having so many Superpowers is conflicting motivations. When one Superpower becomes attached to an idea, it can suppress the input of her other Superpowers. At times, the Container and the Innovator can be at odds with each other. The Container can micro manage the Innovator's time. The Innovator wants to modify without restraint and becomes frustrated with her Container's adherence to schedule. She addresses this internal conflict by hiking in nature to gain perspective. Gia will tune inward to observe her thoughts. This helps her sift through what thoughts are serving her greater good and what thoughts are born from limiting beliefs. Additionally, she will consult with a good listener who can be a neutral sounding board and support her breakthrough.

Another hindrance to Gia's Superpower is physical states of overdoing. When she is exhausted, her creativity is blocked. Her need for rest must outweigh her desire to evolve. She expressed that her downfall in this regard is her "should list." Gia has to prioritize her need for rest and downtime.

Her awareness of others' limiting belief systems also may block her Superpower combinations. When people doubt her insights, it thwarts her creativity as an Innovator and cuts off her reflections as an Observer. When faced with those who have limiting beliefs, she has to release any attachment to their observations.

As we can see from Gia's example we can access several Superpowers to support an intention. Remaining buoyant with each Superpower helps us sustain the journey we are hoping for. As we stay open to modification of our expression of our Superpower combination we become more adept at using the combo each time. As we age with our Superpowers, they blend and integrate into our consciousness actions, attitudes and beliefs.

Conscious Journaling

Read and reflect on the following questions.

Remain open to your first answer to each question.

Write it down so you can see it.

Share the results with someone who is a good listener, or someone who could benefit from knowing you.

ADDING AND COMBINING SUPERPOWERS • 109

1. What Superpowers am I attracted to combine?

2. How can I apply this combination of Superpowers?

3. Who can help mentor/mastermind with me to learn a new Superpower?

4. What kind of journey and outcome do I desire from my Superpower combo?

    a   In my relationships?

b. In my community?

[   ]

c. In my career?

[   ]

Chapter Summary

Jeff and Gia show us different approaches to adding Superpowers to our bank account. When we invest in their growth it impels powerful experiences and outcomes. When we align our Superpowers with our positive thoughts we evolve in our consciousness. Aligning all of our Superpowers to support one, unified intention paves the way for more balanced journeys and favorable landings.

Chapter 17

CORE VIRTUES

"The privilege of a lifetime is to become who you truly are."

—Carl Jung

When mastering and integrating the twelve Superpowers, you also need to access virtues that will nourish your Superpowers. These will assist you in your quest toward actualization.

Once, I struggled with using an online platform to teach an Intuitive Meditation group program. Every time I tested the program by myself, it would work, but every time I taught the class, a distracting glitch derailed me. I was so frustrated and worried my students were disappointed, so I called a friend to help me reset my approach to the problem. He encouraged me to be a scientist and make the class an experiment: take a step back and get a bigger picture about what might make this work. Get curious. This approach released my emotions from the situation so I could reset my approach. When I called in technical support, I was in a better place to explain the glitches so we could test more solutions. The cure was so simple I couldn't believe I overlooked it. Curiosity helped diffuse my emotions so I could ask different questions from a neutral perspective.

The following attributes can generate new pathways to support and accelerate our Superpowers. As you read them, feel free to add more to the list. You are collaborating with this playbook. I invite you to take a deeper dive into what core virtues can enhance your Superpower awakening.

1. Love

The most powerful catalyst in our life is our capacity to give and receive love. We give love to our Superpowers to nourish our relationships, our purpose, and our projects. Allowing our self-love to flourish will increase our passion and enjoyment of life's' gifts. The act of loving our Superpowers AND loving others can encourage them to own and love their Superpowers too.

2. Gratitude

Starting and ending our day with gratitude lightens our mood, provides a positive attitude, and opens our hearts to new modes of being. Expressing appreciation to our colleagues, friends, and family shows how much we value them. It nourishes our need to give and receive from one another. Cultivating gratitude for your Superpowers will increase their effectiveness. Make a point of writing or saying three things you are grateful for each day.

3. Compassion

Our ability to understand and desire to alleviate suffering has many applications. It works in tandem with forgiveness. Compassion can increase our understanding when we are frustrated with our Superpower. It can boost our patience when we sense others are not using their Superpower at maximum capacity. Being compassionate can soften situations when emotions become overwhelming. It buffers any inner or outer conflict with our Superpowers.

4. Forgiveness

When we allow someone mercy, we release destructive negativity. This reconciliation allows us to release others and ourselves from the past. Being willing to acknowledge mistakes redirects our energy toward more productive mindsets. We can admit that life is "a practice," not "a perfect." Forgiveness is an act of extending absolution.

The Hawaiian Ho'oponopono prayer is a powerful forgiveness invocation that essentially means to "make it right." It is made up of four simple sentences:

"I am sorry. Please forgive me. I love you. Thank you." Practice this every time you feel your inner critic weighing you down. It is also a powerful healing balm to relationship wounds. It takes strength to be vulnerable, to forgive ourselves, and to extend that grace to others. Tapping into forgiveness can free up channels of creativity when we feel blocked from our Superpowers.

5. Trust
Aligning with trust opens an abundant flow of prosperous creativity. Trusting we are where we need to be strengthens our Superpower. Trust reinforces our conviction to use and amplify our Superpower.

6. Honesty
When we can admit where we are in the moment, we gain clarity regarding our next steps. Mindful honesty verifies when we need to seek guidance, support, or a shift in mindset.

Thomas Jefferson asserted: "Honesty is the first chapter in the book of wisdom." Acting honestly elevates our Superpower to the next level. Being honest can shine the flashlight on how we may be holding ourselves back.

7. Enthusiasm
When we tap into enthusiasm, we create dynamic momentum toward transformation. We can lean on our friends and support systems to keep our joy quotient full. Enthusiasm can be heightened by switching up routines. Our joyfulness can overcome boredom and apathy. Enthusiasm can spark our Superpower to be used in imaginative ways, igniting a Superpower movement.

8. Love of Learning

When we embrace a beginner mindset, we can learn new concepts about ourselves, expand our knowledge, and acquire new methods. Love of learning directs us to our "aha moments." Technology offers a wide spectrum of learning methods from videos, social media, and online platforms, making knowledge more accessible. Inspired learning keeps our minds supple and brilliant. Applying this virtue can enliven our process of Superpower development.

9. Modesty

Humility releases the ego attachments of being flawless. It opens our minds and hearts to take in new experiences and new ways of being. By being modest, people can hear one another better without bravado/ego taking up the spotlight. Owning our Superpower does not eclipse another's brilliance. There is room at the table for all expressions of Superpowers.

10. Patience

Being patient can alleviate tension and attract other virtues to combine for a greater outcome. Applying patience can help us surrender to our process of strengthening our Superpowers. It takes a prosperous mindset to be patient, and you must trust there will be enough time. Trust and patience partner to unite our Superpowers for lighter journeys and brighter outcomes. Observe how Innovators bridle expectations with patience and modify until they get their desired results.

11. Transcendence

Forging connections to the larger universe provide deeper meaning to our consciousness. People who appreciate the beauty and feel a sense of awe for the natural world experience a deeper level of satisfaction and richness in everyday experiences. We can rise above mundane experiences with transcendence. This empowers our Superpower to dream beyond what we once believed was possible. Remember the phrase "What would it be like if _____?" Our transcendence spurs imagination to fill in the blanks.

12. Resilience

When we dust ourselves off after a fall, we propel our Superpower to change its course. We can be resilient after a disappointing outcome to change our perception of failure. This positive rebound opens our mind to exploring new possibilities of Superpowers.

13. Curiosity

This invites a sense of experimentation with our Superpowers. It is compelled by a desire to "know more completely." Our curiosity is powerful in shifting defeating thoughts to liberating ones. It leads to questions and adventures not yet explored. Using our Observer Superpower allows us to step back from a situation and get curious about our "why." Being inquisitive about our observations can enlighten us. Curiosity can release waves of emotion, opening us to a Superpower breakthrough.

14. Wisdom

Our ability to actualize knowledge, experience and, insight can generate better choices. Wisdom gives birth to change by reminding us we have been somewhere before and it may not serve us to dwell there again. Integrating past experiences with wisdom eases the rough part of transitions.

15. Open-Mindedness

In Yoga, we cultivate a beginner's mind every time we practice. It refines our breath, intention, and postures. Doing so shows us what is truly available for our practice, on and off the yoga mat. When we are open-minded, we release our attachment to specific outcomes and grant ourselves unlimited possibilities. When we keep an open mind, we see potential in our Superpowers and others. Open-mindedness can allow us to see Superpowers we may have overlooked before.

16. Originality

Willingness to share our true selves creates a ripple effect and influences others—it gives them permission to be original. It allows for more spontaneity in brainstorming. We can reinvent how we own and actualize our Superpower. Making your Superpower(s) uniquely yours accesses your greatest resource: your life experience.

17. Courage

Our ability to access new pathways may require us to attempt something we have never tried before. Stepping forward with confidence enables us to progress further. Jumping off the high dive with a new Superpower is possible with extra courage. Courage eases resistance to change. Seeing other Superpowers act with courage can inspire us to reach for the next rung.

18. Willingness to Change

Embracing change with eagerness can make the unknown less daunting. Adopting a cheerful disposition shifts our fear of uncertainty to excitement. Teaming up with other Superpowers for support can magnify our willingness to see what lies beyond the change itself.

19. Humor

Laughter lightens any tension regarding fear and resistance. It keeps us buoyant and allows our Superpower creation to remain light. Humor also helps us enjoy the Superpower breakthrough with others. Laughing gets us out of our head and back into our heart.

20. Altruism

An essential ingredient to spark your Superpower is a profound concern for others. Several of the people I interviewed for this book stated that being of service ignited their Superpower. We are all connected in some way. It makes us feel good to give to others and see others prosper. Imagine how inspiring it would feel to tell someone you see their Superpower in action. Imagine how it might feel to support the growth of Superpowers in a community project. Envision how Superpowers could elevate expansion of consciousness if everyone were in alignment to support each other.

CORE VIRTUES • 117

21. Discernment

Our ability to sort, then choose what Superpowers are essential influences our investment. It also helps us decide which Superpowers to apply for the best journey and outcome.

22. Creativity

Creativity enhances all pathways and expands our problem-solving abilities. Thinking beyond the first idea to an innovative idea impacts our engagement on the journey. You can add variety to your Superpowers' uses with creative applications. Creativity nourishes expansion of original ideas. Imagine ingenious versions of Superpowers to flower beyond their first harvest.

Conscious Journaling

Read and reflect on the following questions.
Remain open to your first answer to each question.
Write it down so you can see it.
Share the results with someone who is a good listener or someone who could benefit from knowing you.

1. What core virtues do I *already* tap into frequently that serve me:
    a. in my relationships?

b. in my life path?

c. in my community?

2. What core virtues do I need to implement to improve my life experiences?

3. What core virtues would help my Superpower?

4. What core virtues could I use to support a friend's Superpower?

5. Who has core virtues do I admire in a friend/mentor that I could emulate?

6. How could I incorporate those desired core virtues into my relationships?

    b. My community?

    c. My life path or career?

7. What is one limiting belief I could release to help me foster a desired core virtue(s)?

Chapter Summary

Core virtues nourish the best versions of our Superpowers. We can incorporate several that align with our desired intention and use of our Superpower. They keep our Superpower on a path of growth and enlightenment. They offer openings to release obstacles and feed inspirational thoughts.

Chapter 18

IMPORTANCE OF INTEGRATION

"What you get by achieving your goals is NOT as important as what you become."

—Henry David Thoreau

Integrating what you learn is just as important as listening to the information. To incorporate your beliefs and Superpowers, you must be willing to give yourself downtime.

How do we block our growth and learning? By never making time to be silent and still. I am talking about over-doers and belief systems driven by thoughts of "not enough." These are poverty-stricken mindsets that drive us beyond our physical and mental capacity. It is essential to take time every day and every week to rest, release, and do nothing. When we are constantly in motion there is no time to receive insights and learning. When you take time to quiet the mind and slow your breath, you are affirming to yourself that you have *plenty* of time to accept new information into your awareness, *and* you discover urgent action items to accomplish. To integrate is to tune into a prosperous mindset.

There are many ways we can embody an experience so it becomes a learned process. Active integration is when you do something repetitive for a certain amount of time; for example, swimming, walking, jogging, driving a beautiful, scenic drive (without traffic lights.) Passive integration is when your mind and body are still, relaxed, and in a posture of receiving. This form of integration is more powerful than active because you are setting yourself up to be a receptacle of insights. By receiving massage, bodywork, acupuncture, or facials, you can reset the mind and body into a more relaxed state. Thermal hydrotherapy (immersing the body in a sauna then immersing in cool water for brief intervals) is another technique that can release tension, allowing your body to rejuvenate.

We set aside 5-10 minutes at the end of every yoga class to allow the body to process all the postures and breaths in *Savasana* or corpse pose. It can be one of the most difficult poses for some people to hold still, breathe quietly, and *not think* during the 5-10 minutes. However, it is a necessary element to accentuate the yoga practice. The brain and neural pathways need this time to allow the alignments of each shape to "sink in." We feel refreshed and awake when we come out of *Savasana*. It allows mind, body and breath to reset to a mindful, yet serene alertness.

Active Integration:
Meditation
Hiking/Swimming/Walking
Talking to a friend
Drinking tea
Gentle yoga
Pranayama (breathing practice)
Journaling
Collaging/Vision Boarding
Reading
Writing a personal letter
Long drive in nature

Passive Integration:
Massage
Bodywork
Acupressure
Acupuncture

Facial
Pedicure/Manicure
Mud-bath
Sauna
Thermal Hydrotherapy (soaking in hot tub or salt bath)
Aromatherapy (Topical Application/Diffusing Essential Oils)
Lying down with an eye pillow and listening to soothing music

Benefits of Integration Meditation
Set yourself up for the following meditation and use it in the future to allow for a full body reset. When to use this meditation:
+after an "aha" moment
+after receiving a mentoring session
+after a class
+after a strenuous day
+after exercise/stretching
+after a brainstorming session
+after you have just learned something new
+to reset the mind, body, and breath prior to an important event
+after yoga
+after a group bonding exercise
+before journaling
+when springing into a new endeavor
+when you are overworked/exhausted

Integration Meditation
- Lie on your back comfortably.
- Have your knees bent with the soles of your feet on the ground. Prop a comfortable pillow supportively under your neck. If you tend toward being cold, then put a light blanket over you.

- Close your eyes and cover them with a soft eye pillow.
- Take slow, deep, and steady breaths.
- Count to four for your inhale; pause, then count the same for your exhale. Pause. (Do five rounds of this measured breathing.)
- Imagine that the bottoms of your feet open and tree roots extend. Now deepen their roots into the soil beneath you. Breathe a full breath.
- Send a third root down from the bottom of your spine. See in your mind's eye the third root anchoring down into the soil near the other two roots. It should look like a tripod. Take another deep breath.
- Feel the heaviness of your body as you relax deeper.
- Feel all your muscles loosen, melt, and release tension with each soothing breath.
- Imagine you are lying on warm sand at a quiet beach. Quiet waves are gently lapping rhythmically on the shore.
- Your breath softens with the pulse of the waves.
- Notice the feeling of tranquility that encompasses your body now.
- Breathe.
- Take a quiet moment to just be in this moment with your breath and your body. (Pause for a minute, then continue)
- You are a powerful visionary who is bringing your creation into being. Invest your highest level of trust in this creation of your breath and your body.
- Take another deep breath and release.
- Gently move your fingers and toes.
- Come back to stillness.
- Take a deep breath, pause for a moment, then exhale the breath.
- Notice the coolness of the air as it comes in your nostrils, then the warmth as it leaves.

- Slowly roll to your side and curl your knees up toward your chest.
- Pause for a slow deep inhale and exhale.
- Gradually push yourself up to a comfortable seated position.
- Gently open your eyes.
- Notice how calm and refreshed you feel now.

Chapter Summary

Integration of learning helps us download knowledge and skills so we can incorporate new Superpowers into our everyday actions, attitudes and beliefs. Passive integration is complete mental and physical surrender to relaxation. Active integration are physical activities that are relaxing or repetitive to open the physical or mental body to assimilate information.

Chapter 19

BREAKTHROUGH

"Breakthroughs happen when limiting thoughts and behaviors are challenged."

—Fabienne Fredrickson

MEDITATE, VISUALIZE, MOVE, AFFIRM

I've divided this chapter into four parts to help you reap the benefits of your Superpower. "Meditate" and "Visualize" are combined with each meditation. The "Move" category offers action steps to initiate change, and the "Affirm" category is packed with phrases to nourish your thoughts.

1. What are some benefits I can expect from doing these exercises?

+Deeper awareness of limiting thoughts and belief systems

+Self-esteem boost

+Clarity of strengths

+Increased motivation to use Superpower

+Increased bonding if done with a group

+Elevated understanding of new Superpowers

2. Which activity should I do for which outcome?

+Always start with activity #1, then look at which outcomes of other exercises match your needs.

3. When is a good time to initiate these activities?

+In the initial creation stage of a project or idea
+When you can open space in your schedule to allow enough time to integrate information (I suggest at least one hour or more)
+Anytime you feel stymied, blocked, or out of the flow.
+Anytime you need to release stress.

4. Where are some optimum places for doing these activities?

+Nature
+A place where you can have space to yourself.
+A quiet, serene setting where you feel completely relaxed.

5. Are there any pitfalls of doing these exercises?

+No, although blocks may be revealed to you.
+Look at these blocks with utmost understanding, patience, and compassion.
+Working through blocks will bring a deeper level of engagement with your Superpower.

6. If I have never meditated before, can I still do this exercise?

+Yes! I have a link to my website where you can access my recording.
+If you find your mind wanders, keep going back to the rhythm of your breath.

7. What benefits can I expect if I practice these meditations regularly (daily/weekly)?

+Greater ease during meditation.
+Being able to maintain positive thoughts in the present moment.
+Increased clarity around which actions, thoughts, and beliefs are working.

+Better awareness of which thoughts, attitudes, and beliefs block you.

+With regular practice, you can start to see faster responses to unexpected outcomes.

+Meditation and deep breathing enhance relaxation.

+Meditation inhibits our stress responses.

+When these meditations are done regularly with a group you can expect people to bond from the shared experience.

MEDITATE AND VISUALIZE

#1 Meditation: Fearless Memory

In this meditation, you will be guided to release fearful thoughts and memories.

Lie down comfortably as you do this meditation with the lights dimmed or off.
Diffuse: Lavender essential oil.
After you complete the meditation, allow yourself to come out slowly.

- Get comfortable lying down on the floor, placing a blanket or rolled up towel under your head and/or under your knees.
- Take the next few moments to tune into the rhythm of your breath.
- Feel the cool air coming in through your nostrils on the inhale, feel the warm air going out on the exhale.
- Allow your breath to expand in your chest, your belly, and your upper back.
- You are getting more and more relaxed.
- Allow your thoughts to pass through your mind as though you were watching clouds pass by in the sky.
- Take another deep breath in and pause, then exhale the breath.
- Imagine you are rooted to the earth like a tree. Picture your feet opening and roots extending from your feet into the earth.
- Breathe.
- Recall a memory of when you felt afraid.
- Notice where you felt that fear in your body, your mind, or your breath.
- See how big or small you are in this memory. Look at your body's shape.
- Observe what the fear felt like in the memory.
- Become aware of your response to fear in that memory.

- In the first moments of your fear, imagine making yourself bigger, stepping toward the fear, and saying to the fear, "I am no longer willing to be a prisoner to you, Fear!"
- Take a deep breath, then say to yourself, "I release any and all of my thoughts and limitations from Fear."
- Now see yourself in the present moment as strong and confident. Step forward into your memory and choose a fearless path.
- Breathe three deep, full breaths.
- Notice how your breath expands into your chest, belly, and upper back.
- Be aware of how completely relaxed you feel.
- Imagine you are grounded like a tree to the earth.
- Bring gentle movements to your fingers and toes. Breathe.
- Slowly become more alert as you gradually open your eyes.

#2 Meditation:

Moving from F.E.A.R. to Excitement

In this meditation, you will be guided to shift fear to excitement.
Lie or sit down comfortably as you do this meditation.
Lights dimmed or off.
Diffuse: Grapefruit, Ylang ylang or Frankincense essential oils
Make sure you are **seated** in a comfortable, relaxed posture and remain alert.

- Tune into your breath. Allow your breath to expand in your belly, chest, and upper back.
- Begin to lengthen your inhale, pause, then exhale the breath.
- Visualize growing roots from the soles of your feet and extending those tree roots deep into the earth.
- Notice how your body begins to relax after visualizing yourself being anchored like a tree.
- Take a deep breath.

- Now place one hand on your belly and one on your chest right below your throat.
- Feel your hands lift on the inhale and fall on the exhale.
- Take a couple deeper breaths.
- Release any limiting thoughts; see them pass by like a leaf floating down a river.
- Now visualize yourself in a new place you have always wanted to go.
- See yourself there with clear details: colors, sounds, smells, textures.
- Imagine yourself performing a new skill you have always wanted to learn. Allow your imagination to expand. Get adventurous.
- Observe any limiting feelings that arise in your body.
- Pour any fearful feelings out of your body as though you had a drain below your feet.
- Observe, then let go of any limiting thoughts inhibiting your experience. Ball them up like a paper wad and throw them out of your mind.
- Feel your hands on your belly and chest as well as your breath.
- Notice any surprising and joyful aspects of your visualization.
- Tune into the excitement of finding unexpected delight in this new skill.
- Tune into the feeling of breath in your hands and excitement in your body.
- Recall your feet rooted to the earth and ground this visualization into your waking path.
- Take a slow, deep breath and sigh.
- Gently wiggle fingers and toes, ankles and wrists.
- Slowly come out of meditation.

#3 Meditation: Cultivating a Confident Mindset

In this meditation, you will be guided to believe in your Superpower.
Sit upright with both feet on the ground.
Use low lighting or soft candlelight.

Diffuse: Wild Orange, Kumquat or Lemon Verbena essential oils.

- Begin by noticing your breath as it comes in and out of your nostrils.
- Allow your breath to expand your belly, ribcage, chest, and upper back.
- Notice the rhythm of your breath.
- Feel your feet on the floor by wiggling your toes. Rotate on the balls of your feet a few times, then relax your feet and ankles.
- Bend and straighten your legs, one at a time, then both simultaneously.
- Slowly shift your weight side to side on your chair a couple of times.
- Maintain your deep, regular breathing in and out of your nostrils.
- Imagine you are standing on a tree-lined path in a place comfortable and familiar to you.
- Visualize your feet placed on gold stepping stones.
- Imagine doing an activity you have been longing to do.
- Take a deep breath.
- Visualize yourself doing this activity with complete joy and strength.
- Allow your thoughts to flood with positive feelings of what you imagine it would feel like.
- Now see your feet walking on each gold stepping stone closer and closer to a movie screen.
- Step into the movie. See yourself as courageous, open to all positive streams of possibilities.
- Feel a warm glow flowing from the center of your chest, radiating through your throat and out the top of your head.
- Feel it radiate down your arms and out your fingers.
- Now feel the warm glow coming from your heart, swiveling down your torso and legs, then streaming out your feet into the earth.

- Imagine the warm, radiant glow melting down to your feet and absorbing into the earth.
- Take a few deep, refreshing breaths in and out your nose.
- Gently wiggle your fingers and toes.
- Slowly come out of meditation.

#4 Meditation: Releasing Limiting Beliefs

In this meditation, you will be guided to let go of any limiting beliefs holding you back from activating your Superpower.
Sit or lie down comfortably with your feet on the floor.
Diffuse: White Fir or Tangerine or Frankincense essential oils.
Keep a soft light or candlelight in the room.

- Close your eyes and notice your breath.
- Breathe in and out of your nostrils slowly, deep and steady 4-5 times.
- Bring your gaze inward to your thoughts.
- Visualize you are planting your feet firmly in the earth and placing your hands on your hips.
- Allow the most recent limiting thought to come to mind (i.e., "I never have enough time, money, resources, health" or "Why would I ever attempt to change? I never can commit to healthy habits.")
- Now say it out loud.
- Observe what it feels like in your body.
- Shrug your shoulders, gently rock your head slowly side to side and release the tension of that thought and those words.
- Take a deep breath and blow out the negativity of your thoughts and words.
- Forgive yourself for holding this thought by saying to yourself, "I am sorry. Please forgive me. I love you. Thank you."

- Name one blessing you received from becoming aware of this limiting belief. Be thankful for your awareness so you can release the limitation.
- Choose a new prosperous, empowering thought.
- See yourself committing to this thought with action.
- Expand your breath to allow positive thinking to envelop you.
- Visualize the positive effects of believing in this new thought.
- Wrap your arms around yourself and breathe in confidence that you can commit to creating change.
- Say out loud three times: "I am capable of great transformation."
- Observe your feelings.
- See yourself being filled inside and out with radiant energy with your feet firmly planted in the earth.
- Breathe.
- Gently move fingers and toes. Slowly come out of meditation.

#5 Meditation: Move Beyond Your Comfort Zone

In this meditation, you will be guided to take steps out of your comfort zone.
Sit comfortably with your feet on the floor.
Remain alert, yet relaxed.
Keep soft, low light or candlelight in the room.
Diffuse: Bergamot, Peppermint and Lime essential oils.

- Close your eyes and take five rounds of full, relaxed breaths in and out of your nose.
- Allow your awareness to focus on the soles of your feet and visualize them opening up like a wide camera lens.
- See roots sprouting from the bottoms of your feet and descending with gravity deep into the earth. Take three full breaths.

- Visualize chalk in your hand, then draw a large circle on the ground around the perimeter of your feet.
- Place words or symbols outside the circle describing an experience you desire but have been afraid to try until now.
- Call in a Superpower or Superpowers to feel confident enough to have this experience: Activator, Amplifier, Observer, Transformer, Expander, Innovator, Synthesizer, Container, Limitless Achiever, Empath, Optimist, Intuitive.
- Affirm and say out loud: "I AM ENOUGH."
- You have everything you need inside of you to step outside this comfort zone.
- Imagine you are wearing a cape with your Superpower written on it.
- See the word "courage" dangling on a necklace over your heart.
- Now stand up and see yourself walking out of the chalk circle.
- Pick up the symbol or words that you placed outside the chalk circle and hold them lovingly in your hands.
- Take three deep breaths and hold this image with stillness.
- Believe in the possibility of having this outcome.
- Become aware of how small the step was outside your comfort zone.
- Gently move fingers and toes, ankles and wrists. Come out of the meditation feeling refreshed and courageous.

#6 Meditation: Affirming the Power of Your Creativity

In this meditation, you will amplify your expression of creativity.
Lie down comfortably on your back with your neck supported and bend your knees so your feet are planted on the floor.
Relax your shoulders and arms, and have your palms face the ceiling in a posture of receptivity.

Utilize soft low light throughout the meditation.
Diffuse: Clary Sage and Ylang Ylang essential oils.

- Close your eyes and slow your breathing.
- Start your inhale from deep in your belly and allow your chest to rise, filling it with air.
- Release the breath slowly on the exhale, feeling your chest fall and your belly hollow out.
- Repeat five times.
- Now imagine yourself in a peaceful place that is meaningful to you.
- Visualize the colors of your surroundings in your mind's eye.
- Feel the temperature of the place.
- Notice the light source and the quality of the light.
- Observe if there are animals present, and if so, the type of movements of the animals.
- What kind of nature surrounds you? What would you like to see?
- Allow your mind to elaborate on the details of this place to make it yours.
- See yourself as peaceful and relaxed in this beautiful place.
- Take three deep breaths, fully relaxing into this place.
- Take notice of your hands.
- Wriggle your fingers and rub your hands together.
- Your hands are constantly giving and receiving energy.
- Offer gratitude to your hands for all they do for you. Think of three blessings you receive with your hands.
- Take a couple of deep breaths.
- Visualize a personal symbol to represent your creativity.
- Be open to whatever symbol comes to mind.

- It could be a color, pen, paint brush, cooking utensil, musical instrument, power tool, journal, microphone, seed, vehicle, butterfly, flower, tree, type of food or beverage.
- Now focus on that symbol in your hands and sense the ways you could use it.
- Imagine there is a waterfall or a garden hose above your head, showering you with ideas of how to collaborate with the symbol.
- Add any ingredients needed to make this scene fun and playful: music, food, animals, colors, people, whatever comes to mind.
- See creative activity sparked by the symbol. Let it flow through your ears like music, enter your nose like oxygen, wash through the rest of your body like water and through your mouth like tasty food.
- Breathe three slow, full breaths.
- Observe the changes in your mind and body from when you first started.
- Gently move fingers, toes, ankles, and wrists.
- Roll to your side and pause for a moment in a fetal position with your knees bent and drawn up to your chest. Pause for a deep breath.
- Slowly push yourself up from the floor.
- Follow your first impulse as a result of this meditation.

MOVE

#1 "Thought Swap"

This activity will help you detox from negative thinking. How often do you say, "I never show up on time... get my office in order... stay in shape...," etc. You say it so often you become immune to hearing it and you become that thought.

Here's the challenge:

- For the next 30 days, wear an elasticized bracelet or ring on one hand.
- When a limiting or fearful thought, phrase, or word comes to mind or out of your mouth, switch the bracelet/ring to the other hand.
- As you swap the bracelet/ring, swap (replace) the limiting/negative thought for a positive, supportive possibility.
- Try and keep the bracelet on one hand for ONE DAY by holding positive thoughts and saying positive words without limiting beliefs.
- Once you have made it through one day, make it through one week, two weeks, all the way to one month.

Note: This works great if you do it with a friend or group because you will keep each other accountable.

Follow up with the next activity: *Act as if* this new thought is already true and happening in your life. This pairs your positive thought with matching actions for optimal results.

#2 Mind Reset: "Act As If"

For the next 21 days, you will use your positive thoughts to enable new actions, *even if* they have not happened yet.

For example, **replace**, "I never drink enough water" with "I drink ten glasses of water daily." **Replace**, "I could never be organized like The Container Superpower," with "I have a practical system that aligns me with keeping my house organized."

All your thoughts, attitudes, beliefs, and actions are an accurate reflection of your positive mindset. If you slip back into negative, habitual thinking, change the bracelet (from exercise #1) to the other wrist as you upgrade to a positive thought. Forgive yourself. Do your Ho'oponopono prayer: "I am sorry. Please forgive me. I love you. Thank you." And remember, life is a practice, and our mistakes can be our greatest teachers.

#3 Individual and/or Group: "Lights, Camera, Action!"

You can do this activity as a visualization, voice recording, or journal entry. Visualize yourself as though you are in a favorite novel, movie, or TV sitcom, using the desired Superpower.

- Choose a current situation you would like to improve or enhance in some positive way.
- What Superpowers could serve your desired outcome?
- You will take on the roles of the director, actor, and camera person.
- As **director,** look at a situation you want to transform right now.
- Decide what needs to be changed: environment, feeling in the air, lighting, how an actor is playing their role, the overall outcome, etc.
- Tell each player in the scene how you want it to be different.
- Include as many Superpowers you need to make this scene play out differently.
- As a **camera person**, manipulate the angles: zoom up close, back up, focus on the big picture, change light settings, notice different aspects of interactions, etc.
- As an **actor/actress,** see how your role is important to the story and choose your course of action with matching thoughts, feelings, and beliefs about the desired Superpower. (Repeat this for as many Superpowers you added to the scene, turning each actor into a Superpower in the scene.)

- Now play out the scene with each new Superpower actor/character with their motivations, actions, and feelings.
- Get specific: What do they say? Feel? Do? Who do they interact with?
- Visualize the desired outcome.
- If something feels off, you are the director: Call Cut! Fine tune the actors, camera angle/point of view, environment, or scene.
- Ask yourself how can you apply this to a real-life situation. List three powerful action steps that would access your Superpower(s).

#4 Prosperity Circle

The Prosperity Circle is a collection of 3-5 people who are committed to creating abundance in thoughts, attitudes, and beliefs.

When we create a community around a concept, we *amplify* the intention with our commitment and presence in the group. We become accountable to each other to hold that positive intention.

Start this group when you need to launch a new Superpower, initiate a new project, or when you feel you need a community to be uplifted.

- Find 3-5 friends, family members, or colleagues and send them three things you are grateful for every day.
- Encourage the members of the circle to send daily affirmations of gratitude to each other. (You cannot repeat blessings you have stated in the past.)

#5 Activity: Superpower Treasure Map

A Superpower Treasure Map is a collage/vision board expressing ideas, concepts, and images representing the Superpower(s) you are cultivating. It is a visually stimulating roadmap to light your path with attributes you want to incorporate in your journey.

Art supplies: a large piece of foam board or cardboard 2X3 feet, glue, scissors, old magazines, colorful tape, gel pens, paint, glitter.

Have relaxing, ambient music playing in the background.

Diffuse: Tangerine and Lavender essential oils.

Time needed: 2-3 hours or you can assemble this over 2-3 days.

- Gather and cut pictures, words, and symbols that accurately reflect the Superpower you are learning to embody.
- Include various settings with you pictured as the Superpower.
- Include affirmations stated in present time with positive words and ones included in the "Affirm" section.
- Create a path on your map with you at the start, then add the steps with pictures, words, and affirmations that will lead you to the treasure of your Superpower.
- Feel free to embellish and continue to add to the map over time as you see environmental reminders of the Superpower.
- Place your map in a visible place to remind you of your light and power.
- Stand back and admire your Superpower creativity.

#6 Activity: Superpower Generosity Blowout

Ready for a challenge now? Good! Get super grateful for your Superpower gifts.

Today you are going to open your path to using your superpower for a greater good *OUTSIDE* your door. You ARE ready!

Start small: Little acts of kindness mean a lot.

The game plan: Bring good feelings to your community using your Superpower.

- Offer to wash your neighbor's car, weed their garden, or ask if there is anything you can do to make their day. Are they too afraid to say yes? Anonymously leave them a plant, flowers, or a token of love.

- Observe if there are senior citizens who would enjoy a visit, need help with their lawn, or need to go grocery shopping.

Get a little more daring:
- Look up three community nonprofits in your area. Pick one cause that could use your Superpower. Find their next scheduled fundraiser and/or benefit and volunteer. Put it on your calendar and show up with your Superpower at the ready.
- Volunteer at your local library and teach someone how to read.
- Help out at the local senior center.

Go BIG:
- Observe what needs improvement in your community or country. Maybe your city or county government could use your expertise. Go to a city council meeting. See what problems they face. See how your Superpower could help them achieve their goals and improve the welfare of your fellow citizens. Run for office.
- Look up countries and communities suffering from hunger, natural disasters or water shortage. Pair up with organizations already planning on helping in those places; many have work-help vacations already built into their framework.

AFFIRM

The definition of "affirm" is to state or assert positively; maintain as true; to express agreement with or commitment to; to uphold and support.

Place affirmations on your mirror, phone, or in your car—you will see them as though they already exist, making it easier to take the right steps to achieve your goals.

The following list of affirmations are applicable to all the Superpowers.
I left space for you to create your own as well.

For Love

I give love to myself.
It is easy for me to give and receive love.
I allow love to guide my thoughts, actions, and beliefs.

For Boundaries

I set loving boundaries by prioritizing my highest health first.
I listen to my body's need for rest, thirst, hunger, and heartfelt connection to others.
I manage the emotional energy of others by listening with neutrality and objectivity.

For Growth

I eagerly take actions essential for my growth.
I am a creative being full of potential.
I love to reinvent myself.

For Gratitude

I am grateful for the daily blessings in my life.
I am thankful for all that I have created.
I appreciate my connection to the field of infinite possibilities.

For Change

I am a vessel flowing with change.
My transformation is a delightful wonder.
It's fun to expand and venture out of my comfort zone.

For Hearing Inner Guidance

I tune into my intuition with ease.
I listen to my inner guidance and take action on it.
My intuition speaks with focus, accuracy, and vision.

For Collaboration

I engage in creative opportunities with others to achieve abundant success.
I brainstorm brilliant ideas with others to create potent outcomes.
I allow myself to see others' gifts and I support collaboration.

For Receiving Feedback

I step back from my emotional reactions to get a different perspective.
I am open to hearing other people's views of me.
I listen to others with empathy, offering a deeper level of understanding within my relationships.

For Goal Completion

I think about what I want to achieve. I take the right action steps, and I am grateful for my achievement.
I stay engaged with my project despite setbacks.
I remain cheerful and buoyant throughout my process of reaching a goal.

For Organization

I maintain a system to keep my office, papers, and living space well-organized.
I live a clutter-free life.
I receive clarity by maintaining a clear space around me.

For Creativity

I allow my creativity to flourish by recording ideas as they come to me.
I allow my creativity to catalyze me to my next stage of evolution.
I pioneer new uses of my creative resources to improve my current experience.

For Courage

I am filled with bravery and determination to step outside my comfort zone.
I acknowledge my fear then I choose to breathe in excitement.
It is fun to face my fears with my bountiful courage.
I surround myself with courageous people who motivate me to be fearless.

ACKNOWLEDGEMENTS

I appreciate all the contributions and downloads of support, guidance, and creation from the field of infinite possibilities. I could not have completed this endeavor without all of these Superpower people in my circle. I am grateful to my family for their support throughout my process of writing this book: my husband, Jean Paul, my Observer (thanks for listening and holding me as powerful throughout this journey), and my daughter—the heart of my heart—Henriette Violet-Rose, my Amplifier of truth. To my parents, Ken and Susan, thank you for modeling all your Superpowers and allowing me to be my best version of my Superpowers. I am grateful for the incredible insights and spiritual wisdom from Mother Nature as this playbook was revealed to me during my hikes at Ft. Ord National Monument.

Big doff of my hat and bow to all my Superpower reps that agreed to be in this book. Thank you for being transparent and willing to inspire others. I appreciate all of my beta readers' feedback: Claudia, Steve M., Gia, Sarah, Deborah, Steve H., and Mary Lou. You all are so generous with your time, feedback, and encouragement. Thank you, Paige Finn, Synthesizer-Innovator-Amplifier, for edits, accountability, laughter, and support. I appreciate the Container and Optimist Superpowers of Ceri in her urging me to be brilliant. To my Innovator-wordsmith, Cynthia: I appreciate how you improved this book with your gentle feedback and literary expertise. Mary Duan, editor/Container, thank you for cutting my adverb addiction to a minimum. Thank you, Terry, for being my Container/proofreader with a stellar sense of humor. I am grateful to the ideas and accountability of my writing buddy, Mary-Lou Rosengren, author of *The Grand Embrace*. I am super grateful for you, Michael, for your editorial expertise and honesty as Innovator at the final stages of this book. Big thank you, Alicia Dunams, for your tips, coaching, exercises and templates from your inspirational "Best Seller in A Weekend" workshop. Furthermore, Alicia, I appreciate your belief and support of my Superpower movement. You are the Activator I needed to push me out of my comfort zone. Namaste.

BIBLIOGRAPHY

"10 Keys for Happier Living." Accessed November, 2016, http://www.actionforhappiness.org

"Assessment" and "About Archetypes", Accessed November, 2016, http://www.capt.org

Definition of "Traction," Accessed September, 2016, http://www.dictionary.com

"Character Strengths and Virtues: A Handbook and Classification," Peterson, C. and Seligman, M.E.P. (2004), Accessed September, 2016, http://www.viacharacter.org

Pam Grout, *Thank and Grow Rich*, (Hay House, Inc., 2016) p.64.

Marianne Williamson, *Return to Love,* (New York: Harper Collins, 1992), Chapter 7, p.190.

RESOURCES

This is the contact information for the Superpower people I interviewed earlier in this book:

Chapter 1: What is a Superpower?
Steve McMillan, www.smcleadership.com, smcleadership@gmail.com

Chapter 2: The Twelve Superpowers Defined
Activator: Sam Patel, owner, Ike's Place, www.ilikeikesplace.com, svp36@hotmail.com

Amplifier: John Koza, www.camerata-singers.org, johnkoza@comcast.net

Transformer: Lisa McCardle, www.LisaMcCardle.com, Lisa@LisaMcCardle.com

Innovator: Cynthia Shidner, www.learningistalking.blogspot.com, cshidner@gmail.com,

Expander: Donna Aikens, donna@commonbond.biz

Synthesizer: Rob Horgan, ingrid_dv@att.net

Empath: Donna Luder, www.donnaluder.com, donna@donnaluder.com,

Limitless Achiever Saba Moor-Doucette, www.sabasfitforlife.com, saba@sabasfitforlife.com

Intuitive: Heidi Diouf, www.heididiouf.com, heidi@heididiouf.com, 831.521.8123

Chapter 4: How to Approach Failure
Jeff Doucette, doucettejd@aol.com

Chapter 5: Adding and Combining Superpowers
Gia Dimatteo, L.Ac.: owner, Resonance Spa and Wellness, www.resonancemarin.com, 415.891.3328

www.ingramcontent.com/pod-product-compliance
Lightning Source LLC
Chambersburg PA
CBHW082040230426

43670CB00016B/2720